Deadly Betrayal:

The Kidnapping and Murder of McKay Everett

D1605619

Deadly Betrayal:

The Kidnapping and Murder of McKay Everett

Paulette Everett–Norman, M.S.
James W. Marquart, Ph.D.
Janet L. Mullings, Ph.D.

Texas Review Press
Huntsville, TX

FIRST EDITION, 2007

Requests for permission to reproduce material from this work
should be sent to:

Permissions
Texas Review Press
English Department
Sam Houston State University
Huntsville, TX 77341-2146

Cover design by Paul Ruffin

Library of Congress Cataloging-in-Publication Data

Everett-Norman, Paulette.
  Deadly betrayal : the kidnapping and murder of Mckay Everett
/ Paulette
Everett-Norman, James W. Marquart, Janet L. Mullings.
    p. cm.
  ISBN-13: 978-1-881515-98-2 (pbk. : alk. paper)
  ISBN-10: 1-881515-98-2 (pbk. : alk. paper)
  1. Everett-Norman, Paulette. 2. Parents of murder victims--Texas
--MontgomeryCounty--Biography. 3. Everett, McKay, 1983-1995.
4. Murder--Texas--Montgomery County--Case studies. 5. Trials
(Murder)--Texas--Montgomery County--Case studies.
I. Marquart, James W. (James Walter), 1954- II. Mullings, Janet L.
III. Title.
  HV6533.T4E94 2006
  364.152'3092--dc22
                                    2006029794

Table of Contents

Publisher's Note:

A few years ago I received a call from Paulette Everett asking whether I might be interested in helping her write a book on the kidnapping and murder of her son, McKay Everett. I remembered the case very well, so I agreed.

I spent several months converting Paulette's journals into book form, editing as I went, but there was one particular issue that the two of us couldn't agree on, so we decided that it might be better for her to find someone else to help her with the book.

While I was working on the project, I happened to mention it to my graduate creative writing class one night, and a member of the class said that he'd like to talk to me about it. The fact was that Tannie Shannon had been interviewing Hilton Crawford for months in hopes of writing a book on the crime from Crawford's perspective.

I thought that quite a coincidence, and I immediately saw the potential for Texas Review Press. If I released a book on the crime from Paulette's perspective and one from Crawford's, we would have a pair of books that should make a real impact on the Houston/Conroe/Huntsville areas and perhaps the state at large. After all, this was one of the most sensational cases in the history of Texas. Further, it is seldom that you get books from the perspective of both the criminal and the victim (and Paulette, though not directly touched by Crawford, was indeed a victim in this crime).

I issued a contract to Shannon, and he began writing his book, *Seed of Villainy: The Hilton Crawford Story*. Meanwhile, Paulette teamed up with James Marquart and Janet Mullings of the SHSU Department of Criminal Justice, and they prepared a manuscript for me to take a look at it. I liked it and, after receiving approval from the university attorney's office on both manuscripts, I agreed to publish it.

Deadly Betrayal and *Seed of Villainy* are companion books, so if you haven't bought the other one, go buy it. See both sides of the story.

One other thing: Paulette provided me with several photographs of McKay. I thought that the best way to keep the focus on the child was to scatter the shots throughout the book.

—Paul Ruffin, Director, Texas Review Press

Foreword

American society is awash with programs and stories about crime and justice. Big-screen movies and television dramas portray crimes, criminals, investigations, and trials from various angles and story lines. The print media, television, and radio talk shows are also dominated by reportage on sensational crimes. On a positive note, Americans today know more about the criminal justice system than ever before.

On the negative side, Americans know little about victims. Television programs and movies devote most of the story and dialogue to solving the case, or catching the bad guys. While victims do receive some attention, their screen time is severely limited. The vast majority of true-crime books also focus inordinately on the crime, criminal, investigation, and on final resolution of the case.

We, Professors James W. Marquart and Janet L. Mullings at Sam Houston State University, have studied crime and criminals, for over twenty years. We have also taught in the area of criminal justice for two decades. The combined result of our research and teaching has led us to two universal facts: One, we know very little about the long-term effects of violent crime on victims; and two, victims have been given short shrift by researchers, authors, the media, and the entertainment industry.

Deadly Betrayal: The Kidnapping and Murder of McKay Everett is a book that will focus attention on the victim. Each year there are tens of millions of crimes committed in our society. There is at least one victim for each crime committed. Unfortunately, there are often multiple "victims" for every recorded crime. Now is the time to begin to understand how and in what ways "true crime" affected the survivors. *Deadly Betrayal* promises to do just that.

As part of a research project examining the long-term consequences of victimization, in February 2004, we established an "800" number and sent public service announcements to radio stations, police departments, and district attorney offices throughout Texas. We sought recent violent-crime victims to explain, from their view, the impact violent crime had on their lives. We became intrigued by the way in which they were treated by the criminal justice system. Our review of the written research failed to uncover one account of how a victim's case from their perspective traversed the entire criminal justice system, from the moment of the crime, to an arrest, to a trial, a sentence, and eventual parole and beyond including their thoughts and feelings about surviving a violent criminal event.

We listened to the victims retell their horrific stories and searched for the "best" case to examine a wide variety of issues. Issues that ordinary people could relate to may be not for themselves but for people or victims they have known. In late spring 2004, we came into contact with Paulette Norman (Everett), who shared with us a manuscript she had drafted about the kidnapping and murder of her twelve-year-old son, McKay Everett. We reworked the original manuscript to produce *Deadly Betrayal*.

McKay was kidnapped on September 12, 1995, held for ransom, and murdered September 13, 1995. The offender, who was arrested September 15, 1995, was Hilton Crawford, a long-time family friend. McKay, who loved Hilton and even called him "Uncle Hilty," was betrayed—hence the title of our book, *Deadly Betrayal*. McKay's kidnapping, reminiscent of the infamous Nathan Leopold and Richard Loeb kidnapping murder case in 1924 and the Lindbergh baby kidnapping case in 1932, shocked the state of Texas and the nation. How was it possible that an adult could betray the trust of a child? Kidnapping is a rare crime, and when it does occur, it typically involves a parent. Our case involved a family friend, perhaps the rarest form of all kidnapping.

Paulette has willingly agreed to allow the light of systemic analysis to illuminate her case. This exemplary story allows the reader to understand how the case traversed through the criminal justice system from the day the crime was committed, to arrest, trial, appellate history, and final justice. Hilton Crawford was executed in Texas by lethal injection on July 2, 2003. A quirk in the state's criminal justice system allows victims to observe the execution of the condemned, and Paulette Norman witnessed Hilton's execution. She saw and experienced final justice for her son's killer.

Deadly Betrayal is the first book of its kind to fully

examine the long-term consequences of violent crime on victims and their family. We simply do not know if it is possible to "move on." These cases are different from robbery, non-capital murder, or sexual-assault cases. Death is different, and capital cases take years to wind their way through the system. *Deadly Betrayal* shows the reader why death penalty cases take years to reach closure. We also examine what it is like for victims to come face-to-face with their child's killer in the death chamber.

Deadly Betrayal is a work of original research that employs the observations of the victim's mother, trial transcripts, and interviews with key players in this tragedy to examine a kidnapping and murder case, including execution. Five themes are examined: 1) kidnapping—murder; 2) the long-term effects of violent crime on a family; 3) the "place" of victims in the criminal justice process; 4) betrayal and greed; and 5) final justice. *Deadly Betrayal* is the first true-crime book to handle each of these themes in language easily understood by ordinary readers.

Professors Marquart and Mullings have spent the last five years examining child maltreatment as a violent crime. We recently published a two-volume set of scholarly articles on the victimization of children, and these articles were combined into a book published by Haworth Press. We are also professors of criminal justice and routinely teach students about police, courts, and corrections. *Deadly Betrayal* is about a unique form of child victimization that involved the police, courts, and correctional system.

The only other situation involving the issues previously described occurred in the Oklahoma City bombing with the subsequent execution of Timothy McVeigh. We fully expect that within the next 12 to 24 months, other authors and victims of this bombing will present similar stories examining the same issues discussed in this proposal, but *Deadly Betrayal* is the first. Indeed, this book provides a structure for other victims to follow and, with time, we will be able to develop a coherent picture of the long-term consequences of violent victimization, as well as how victims survive and cope with their loss.

Our book can assist victims and non-victims to understand the effects of violence on themselves, friends, communities, and the criminal justice system. On a larger level, even terrorism (Oklahoma City Bombing) is, in reality, a violent crime. This book also provides insights into the process of survival that would benefit these victims. We are ahead in our analysis and are paving the way for a better understanding of the consequences of violence.

Deadly Betrayal fits in well with the recent publishing trend about human survival and resiliency. The Everetts were essentially the "family next door" and McKay was the "kid next door." They were ordinary people affected by an extraordinary crime, but they survived. Paulette has resumed her primary teaching career and currently speaks to groups about grief, trauma, and survival. This crime and her will to survive will be of interest to ordinary readers. *Deadly Betrayal* will also find a home in high school and college classes.

—The Authors

Introduction: Through a Mother's Eyes

The sun had just set over the horizon and the flood lights turned on to reveal a green field and incredibly smooth brown dirt. It was the green field, though, that caught everyone's attention. The grass was so green it didn't look real. The grandstand was packed full of people. Some people in the crowd were intently studying their programs and talking quietly with friends. They talked in hushed tones and looked around to see if anybody was eavesdropping. These folks were acting as if they were trading state secrets or had a line on something really big. Others in the grandstand were eating, drinking, and laughing as they traded binoculars for glasses of beer. The binoculars were drawn to the green infield and smooth brown dirt. Most of the people, though, were running from the aisles to find a seat. The game was about to begin, and everyone was clearly excited.

The grandstand was perched high above the infield, and the rows of seats were arranged steeply to allow a clear view of the action. The stands looked out over the oval track, and on cue every head looked left at the post parade or the horses and jockeys moving past the stands to the starting gate.

It was July 1995 in Bossier City, Louisiana, and even though the race was at 9:00 p.m., it was still blistering hot. The metal grandstand at Louisiana Downs absorbed the day's heat, and the horses and jockeys were "sweating bullets" as they say in the South. The heat made the track dry and even, which made for a fast race. This was a stakes race and a lot of money had been bet. As in a pool hall, the smell of money, and gambling brought out the experts. "Don't back a horse that's being asked to do something he's never done before." "Forget about #7, he's a morning glory, you know, he runs good in training but can't finish a real race." Advice, advice, lots of advice was being thrown around by the track regulars and wannabes. The problem was that few people were listening to these self-proclaimed experts. The horses moved into the starting gates. "Forget about #2, he's a lug, got no endurance."

Without any notice, the loud speakers barked, "And they're off." One horse jumped out as the front runner and tried to stay in the lead around the first turn. His backers cheered. Too bad, though, his lead lasted what seemed like seconds and then another horse surged ahead, followed by another, and then another. Around the track they raced and then the horses moved into the stretch. The jockeys began to use their crops to get more speed out of their rides. The horses rushed towards the finish line. There were shouts of support for each horse. The horses were frenzied, and so were the spectators. The smell of money was in the air.

Then in the last 100 feet a "closer" or late runner surged ahead and won the race. It was a great race, a great performance, and the crowd leaped out of their seats and took off for the betting windows. "I won", "We placed", "Mine showed," a few people told their friends. To a novice or bystander, the race and the action in the grandstand were both fascinating and intoxicating. Thousands of dollars were won and lost within a few minutes.

A man in a yellow golf cap yelled out, "I just won a couple hundred!" and somebody else lamented, "Crap, I just lost two grand again, man; if I can't break even tonight, my old lady's leaving me."

Gambling, it's a risk, it's a skill, it's an art form, and it's fun all in one. Boil all the water out of it and gambling can also become a dangerous habit. Some people worship gambling and its risks. Such people are drawn to it like a moth to a flame and it becomes an addiction, an obsession. In some cases, gambling takes over a person's life and consumes his time, property, and savings. He borrows more to gamble more, to take another shot at a big payday. Some people keep at it until they lose their houses, their families, their friends, and, in extreme cases, even their lives.

The horses were returning to the paddock or stable area, and the crowd readied itself for the next race. More money was in the air. The man who had lost several thousand on the last race told a friend whom he owed money, "Just gimme some more time. I promise to pay you. If I don't get the money I'm gonna kill myself, or somebody." The man looked scared and, worse, he looked as if he meant every word of it. He was serious because he owed some people a lot of money, several hundred thousand dollars.

The debtor's name was Hilton Crawford, and in September 1995 he took his desperate obsession with gambling and debts to the final zone. He kidnapped a young boy named McKay Everett and held him for ransom. He demanded $500,000 from the boy's parents, or else. The "or else" in this case, as in all other kidnappings, meant murder. And when the money didn't come, Hilton brutally murdered the boy, a good friend's child, in a Louisiana swamp.

When we think of murder, we usually think of the mean streets in some rundown area of a big city. We also think of minority victims killed by minority killers over small change, or a verbal slight, killed for next to nothing. That's not the picture here. Our murderer was a white man in his late fifties, an ex-cop, an ex-deputy sheriff, a former little league baseball coach who lived in Conroe, Texas, a suburb of Houston. Hilton had a good life. He had a wife who taught grade school, two sons, and house with a pool. His victim, a twelve-year-old white boy, also lived in Conroe. His parents, Paulette and Carl Everett, had done well in the oil and gas business. Paulette taught grade school. Life was good for McKay Everett also, until Hilton Crawford kidnapped and murdered him during the second week of September 1995.

In that week, McKay Everett, the beloved son of Carl and Paulette, became an American statistic. In 1995 Americans reported almost fourteen million crimes to the police; two million of these were violent crimes. Out of these crimes, Americans also committed 22,000 murders, or roughly sixty per day, about one murder in each state every day. Murder in America happens every day and for wildly diverse reasons. Americans kill each other over debts, perceived wrongs or disrespect, for profit, for personal gain, for sexual hangups, and sometimes just for the hell of it. Double murders occur, and triple murders are not out of the ordinary, nor are mass murders, or even the murder of dozens of victims over time by a serial killer.

On a positive note, almost two-thirds of all murders are cleared by an arrest, which means that the police catch most of the killers. Our criminal justice system devotes enormous resources to solving murders. Research on murder also shows that males are far more likely than females to be both the victims and the offenders. Only a handful of all murder victims are less than fourteen years of age. Interestingly, the most likely precipitating event for a murder is an argument or some spat. This leads to the most well-known fact about murder, that the vast majority of victims and offenders know each other. Murder by a complete stranger is, in the scheme of all crimes committed in the United States, a rare event.

While simple arguments are the primary catalyst for many murders, murder is also known to occur in the course of another felony, more commonly called felony murder. Armed robbers in some instances kill the victim who fights back or tries to protect himself or his property. The correct terminology for such crimes is called murder in the course of a robbery. In general, about sixteen percent of all murders are committed during the commission of another felony.

Perhaps the rarest of all felony murders to occur involves murder in the course of a kidnapping. Kidnapping, by itself, is uncommon. For example, in 2003, reported crime statistics in Texas indicate that there were 185,299 incidents of family violence and 97 percent of all these cases of family violence involved assaults. But less than one percent of these crimes involved kidnapping. Kidnapping happens infrequently, and when kidnappings and murders intersect, extraordinary efforts are employed to solve these cases.

Kidnappings, or abductions, precipitate immense publicity and requests by family members and friends for the safe return of their loved ones. Kidnappings that result in murder inflame and terrify the public. When victims are defenseless children, these crimes quickly become national tragedies or "crimes of the century." One of the most famous kidnapping-murders occurred on May 21, 1924, when fourteen-year-old Bobby Franks was snatched off a quiet street in a well-to-do Chicago neighborhood and murdered by Nathan Leopold, aged twenty, and Richard Loeb, aged twenty-one. The victim's body was mutilated and stuffed in a drainpipe by a lake. Both killers came from wealthy families, were well-educated, and had exceptional IQs. Loeb had graduated from the University of Michigan at age seventeen, and Leopold had graduated from the University of Chicago at eighteen.

The murder of young Franks was in reality a thrill killing, and was a crime that shocked and scared the nation. The public's outrage and fear stemmed from the fact that the teenage victim could have been anyone's child plucked off the street almost at random. So dastardly evil was this crime that it was labeled "The Crime of the Century" and the prosecution argued for the gallows. Leopold and Loeb were defended by the famous attorney Clarence Darrow, who later gained additional celebrity status in 1925 with his performance in *Tennessee vs. John Scopes*, or the "Monkey Trial." Darrow, in his brilliant and emotional twelve-hour summation, argued for the killers' lives; ultimately they received life sentences.

On March 1, 1932, in another celebrated case, someone entered the second floor of famed aviator Charles A. Lindbergh's country estate in New Jersey and kidnapped Charles Jr., a twenty-month-old baby. A ransom note demanded $50,000 for the safe return of the baby. On May 12, 1932, the baby's remains were found in the woods near the Lindbergh home. The infant had died of a skull fracture. An intense investigation ensued, led by Col. H. Norman Schwarzkopf of the New Jersey State Police, father of General Norman Schwarzkopf of Desert Storm fame. Two years later Bruno Hauptmann, a thirty-five-year-old illegal German immigrant, was arrested for another "Crime of the Century." The entire nation grieved for the famed aviator and his wife while newspapers and radio stations warned the public to be wary of strangers. If such a crime could happen to a hero, it could happen to anyone.

Hauptmann was found guilty of the kidnapping and murder in February 1935 and executed fourteen months later on April 2, 1936, in the electric chair at Trenton State Prison. He went to his death refusing to confess. This case remains swirled in controversy to this day. The crime shocked the nation and led Congress to enact, in 1932, the federal kidnapping statute, which facilitated FBI involvement in these crimes.

Twenty years later, in September 1953, six-year-old Bobby Greenlease was taken from his school in Kansas City, Missouri, by Bonnie Heady, who posed as the boy's aunt. Heady explained to school officials that Mrs. Greenlease had suffered a heart attack and requested to see Bobby. They left in a taxi cab and were dropped off a short time later in downtown Kansas City. Carl Hall, Heady's drinking partner, picked up the boy and Heady and drove west of Kansas City, Kansas, to a farm. Here, Hall pistol-whipped Bobby into unconsciousness and then shot him in the head, killing him instantly.

The Greenlease family received ransom demands, but the child's body was found by FBI agents in October 1953. Heady and Hall were arrested, tried in Federal Court, and found guilty of the kidnapping and murder. The motive for the gruesome crime was money. It took the jury a matter of minutes to assess the punishment as death. On December 18, 1953, less than a hundred days after the crime was committed, Heady and Hall were blindfolded and executed together in a "double-header" in the gas chamber, which was equipped with two metal side-by-side chairs, at the Missouri State Penitentiary. This was, after all, the 1950s, and death row prisoners had little recourse in the courts. In these years, justice was typically swift and without fanfare. Lengthy appeals, cries of extenuating circumstances, and experts on human behavior were not yet evident in capital cases. The time between conviction and execution at this time was typically less than twelve months.

On July 4, 1956 one-month-old Peter Weinberger was snatched from his home on Long Island. It was a middle-class home in a quiet neighborhood populated by working folks. Again labeled "the crime of the century," the kidnapping shocked the nation and struck fear in the hearts and minds of average Americans. The case eerily resembled the Lindbergh kidnapping.

Baby Weinberger was no celebrity—he was the product of average parents in "any town" America. The Federal Bureau of Investigation conducted an exhaustive handwriting analysis of the ransom note and found and arrested 31-year-old Angelo LeMarca in August 1956. LeMarca, who had abducted and murdered the child, said he needed the ransom money to pay personal bills as some loan sharks were making threats. He was executed in Sing Sing's electric chair in August 1958. The Weinberger case also led to the new federal legislation that reduced the FBI's waiting period to intervene in kidnapping cases from seven days to 24 hours.

Who would take a child from his parents? Why would someone kill a child for money? Who would betray a child? Kidnapping and murder are indeed uncommon events and often involve very different dynamics and motives. Modern research on kidnapping shows that stranger kidnappings are the least common of kidnappings, followed by acquaintance kidnappings; the most common kidnapping involves adult family members. When family members steal one of their own, the child's house is typically the scene of the crime. In the vast majority of family kidnappings, no weapon is used to take the child. Only a small percentage of all kidnappings result in injuries, and fatalities are extremely rare. Further, forty-one percent of all family kidnappings occur between 6 p.m. and midnight.

Kidnapping arouses the fury for justice in Americans, especially among those people with children. They also unleash the full power of our law enforcement community. Everything is done, every stone turned, and every lead acted upon vigorously to bring the victim home, safe and alive. Most child abductions, in fact, end up this way. The family is traumatized, but whole, and every bed at night is once again occupied, to the relief of parents.

In 1995, mass murder in Oklahoma City occupied the headlines of most American newspapers and nightly news programs. However, in modest Conroe, Texas, in the same year a crime occurred that paralleled the Leopold and Loeb, Lindbergh, Greenlease, and Weinberger crimes. The crime involved the betrayal and brutal murder of young McKay Everett by Hilton Crawford, a "family member" whom McKay adoringly called "Uncle Hilty." McKay was not forcibly removed from his own home. He was taken from his own home, out the back door, at night, and without a struggle. The home was located in an upscale subdivision in northwest Conroe, a town just a few miles north of Houston, Texas. Conroe also happened to be in Montgomery County, and was the county seat.

McKay, like Bobby Franks, Baby Lindbergh, Bobby Greenlease, and Baby Weinberger, did not come home. His bed remains forever empty. September 12, 1995, was a day that forever changed the lives of Carl, Paulette, and McKay Everett, and Hilton Crawford's family. Like most years, 1995 started out with promise for the Everetts, but the events that took place in September 1995 sent the year into a deadly tailspin. The kidnapping of McKay Everett, soon called the "Crime of the Century," was eerily reminiscent of the earlier "crimes of the century" involving the child victims Bobby Franks, Baby Lindbergh, Bobby Greenlease, and Baby Weinberger.

Carl and Paulette, like the horrified parents of those other dead children from long ago, were the victims of the worst crime of all, betrayal. The betrayal of McKay Everett by Hilton Crawford was nothing new in the annals of human history.

Cain sensed he was not in God's favor and, feeling betrayed, he killed his brother Abel. Delilah betrayed Samson for money and love. Brutus betrayed his friend Julius Caesar to save Rome. Judas betrayed his friend and teacher, Jesus, for thirty pieces of silver. In the movie *The Godfather*, Fredo Corleone out of misplaced loyalty betrayed his brother Michael.

There is also something about betrayal that makes it dangerous for those who betray. You might be able to get away with stealing or even murder, but you can not get away with betrayal. Betrayal is not a crime in the legal sense. If betrayal were against the law, many people would be in jail. There is no reprieve, however, from betrayal in the court of everyday life. It seems as though those who practice this foul deed get what is coming to them at some point in time. It may take years to right the wrong, but you just can not get away with betrayal. Everyone knows that Cain, Delilah, Brutus, Judas, and Fredo all disappeared from history, some violently, some quietly. No matter how, they all went away.

Looking back in history, the walls of the pyramids, ancient Chinese texts, the Bible, the plays of Shakespeare, modern books, and every society's collections of folktales and myths recount stories involving betrayal. It is the stuff of everyday and international relations. Most examples of betrayal involve adults, one adult betraying another for whatever reason. Rarely do we encounter an adult intentionally and maliciously betraying and harming a child. It is within the realm of fairy tales that we see children betrayed and harmed by adults.

In the tale of Little Red Riding Hood, children hear about the youthful Little Red, who is almost devoured by the older, craftier wolf. In this tale, youthful trusting innocence was nearly undone by an adult predator. The message in these stories warns children to beware, to be cautious of wolves in sheep's clothing. Fairy tales have for centuries been important literary and oral devices with which to warn the young about potential harm at the hands of their elders. Indeed, it may be polite to respect and even adore one's elders; however, it may not always be prudent to blindly trust them. The irony of childhood is discerning or learning which adults, including friends and strangers, can be trusted and which need to be feared and avoided. Surviving childhood unscathed is no easy task.

Yet, the story of the vicious wolf warns children to

fear strangers, and "Don't talk to strangers" has become the Eleventh Commandment that all danger lurks outside a child's circle of relatives and friends. Sometimes the predator is near, so near that it is invisible. We do not have any fairy tales where the moral warns children about the wolf in their own house or where the danger lies in the body of an aunt or uncle.

When Judas kissed Jesus, the act or moment of betrayal took seconds, but their relationship developed over months and years. In the examples discussed earlier, those betrayed were brothers, lovers, or deep friends. These betrayers did not intentionally ingratiate themselves with and intentionally set up their victims. Instead the relationship between betrayed and betrayer was real and very close. So close and trusting that the victim barely knew what happened. Realization came, but too late.

Betrayal is a dirty deed because it violates trust. The only way to comprehend what happened to the Everetts and the foul deed committed by Hilton Crawford is to see it through a mother's eyes, a survivor's eyes, because only a survivor could explain it to the rest of us.

—Paulette Everett-Norman

Deadly Betrayal:
The Kidnapping and Murder of McKay Everett

"In this century, and moment, of mania. Tell me a story."

—Robert Penn Warren

Chapter 1

Out the Back Door

God, I loved that home. Carl and I, we worked so hard to make it, to get to a place where you could really focus on building something, to sink down roots. We wanted a house and a home. We wanted to give McKay a place to play in, and to grow up in. I liked to design things, and I put a lot of my energy into making that place a real home. I loved to plant things too. McKay and I planted many of the bushes and even the mimosa trees. He just loved the spring, when the flowers and bushes bloomed. He loved the mimosa trees, and he would stick his nose in the blooms and come away with pollen on his face. Oh, the smell of those blooms in the spring—I can remember how he loved to smell the blossoms. Every time I see a mimosa tree now, I can still smell the beautiful blooms. I can see McKay running around the yard. We all loved that house. It was in a nice neighborhood and we had great neighbors. We all got along. We thought it was safe—you know, where the kids could play outside all day and we didn't have to worry about a thing. Funny, I always knew we were safe from strangers.

The house was situated on a street corner on three wooded acres. It was a handsome two-story Southern home with a well-manicured lawn and lots of shrubs, especially azalea bushes. The paint even seemed fresh. It looked as if the owner walked around with a brush and paint can to keep the place looking new. Southerners take their landscaping seriously, and this place was no exception. Mimosa trees dotted the edged lawn. The lush yard was a postcard of beauty in the springtime. Even the address, 431 Pine Springs Court, suggested a place in the forest.

The house was built just far enough off the streets, away from the cars, to inform the casual visitor that privacy was valued here. Not the remoteness of a cabin buried deep in a forest by itself, but enough distance from the street that visitors to the home had to have a purpose for being there. The people who built this place knew what they were doing.

The neighborhood where the home on the corner lot was located was quiet, and most of the parents knew each other and looked after one another's kids. Block parties were common. In the summer months the neighborhood kids were usually outside tossing balls around, riding their bicycles, or running through the woods. The house and its lots and trees in the quiet neighborhood seemed like an oasis, a safe corner in the midst of a rapidly growing metropolitan area.

There was a driveway in front, but the people who lived there liked to use the back entrance. A tree-lined lane snaked its way through the lot to the garage and the back door. Here the family entered and left the house. Visitors reported in at the front door. Family and friends always used the rear entrance. Most houses were like that—front doors were for strangers or occasional guests, and side or back doors were for the regulars.

It was around 10:30 p.m. on September 12, 1995, and Carl Everett was preparing to leave the Village Inn Restaurant in Conroe. He and Paulette were with friends, having coffee after an Amway meeting downtown. Carl had called home several times during the meeting and while at the restaurant to check on McKay, their twelve-year-old son. It was a rainy evening, and he had wanted to make sure McKay was all right.

It bothered Carl that McKay hadn't answered his calls, but he was not alarmed. After all, McKay was nearly a teenager, and kids at this age could be and usually were unpredictable. Besides, it was late and it was a school night, so McKay had to be around the place. Maybe, Carl thought, he was out back. Or he was next door, visiting the neighbors. Nevertheless, he was concerned that there had been no answer to his calls, so his goal was to get home. Before he left, he calmly reassured Paulette and their friends that everything was okay, that there had to be some rational explanation as to why McKay had failed to answer the phone.

Conroe was easy to get around. The trip from the restaurant to their home usually took about ten minutes. Tonight was no different, and Carl was soon turning into their subdivision. As he made his way home, he saw that the lights were on at the house. This was a good sign. Everything on the outside appeared normal. As usual, Carl pulled into the back entrance driveway and parked his truck in the driveway. Even though the house had a three-car garage, he often left his truck in the driveway.

Carl was in the oil and gas business, and he had his own company. Paulette ran the office part of the business. In the 1970s they had come to Texas from Mississippi to start a new life and grab their own piece of the rainbow. They flourished, and the house that they had built on the corner lot symbolized their remarkable success. But their proudest accomplishment was McKay. A beautiful boy, with a light olive complexion, he was a sensitive child, an only child, and he was everything that Carl and Paulette had hoped and prayed for.

With McKay in their lives, Carl and Paulette were rich—they had everything they had ever needed or wanted. Their lives were full now, and they gladly spent long hours to provide for McKay. That was their goal in life as parents: to provide things and opportunities for their child that they had not had when they were growing up in Mississippi. By this measure, the Everetts were successful parents. Because McKay was an only child, he grew up around adults, he socialized with adults, he liked adults, and he trusted adults. The three were, as they say, "pretty tight."

As Carl got out of his truck, he happened to notice that the back door to the house was slightly open. This was odd, very odd, because the house had an alarm system. For the door to be open, McKay would have to have turned off the security system. *Why*?

McKay had grown up with strict orders never to turn off the security system when he was home by himself. In this regard, he was meticulous. He was also the most knowledgeable person in the house when it came to operating the security system. One time the alarm went off at a neighbor's and a police officer came to investigate. The officer knocked on the Everetts' door, but the little boy behind the door refused to open it, even for a police officer. The boy knew better than to open the door for a stranger.

Carl pushed the door open all the way, and he called out for McKay: "Hey, little buddy, where are you?"

He walked through the house calling out for McKay, but his little buddy did not answer. Maybe, Carl thought, McKay was playing hide and seek. The boy could hide anywhere. Carl sensed, however, that something was not right, and he was in no mood for kids' games. It was late and McKay, a seventh-grader, needed to get to bed on this school night.

The house was eerily quiet. McKay was, as Carl quickly realized, not there. He was nowhere around. And then the silence was startled by the ringing of the phone. It was 11:00 p.m., and Carl rushed to answer it. He picked up the phone, thinking and hoping he was going to hear a familiar voice. He was wrong. The stranger's voice on the other end was gruff and harsh: "We've got your son."

At first, Carl thought that the call was a prank, as anyone might. But the caller hissed out demands for a ransom and a warning not to notify the police, or the Everetts would never see their son alive again. The warning to avoid the police erased Carl's doubts about the validity of the call. The conversation lasted only a few minutes, but it left Carl numb. After the line went dead, he ran around the house and yard calling for McKay. There was no answer.

Shortly after Carl called 911 to report the kidnapping, local law enforcement officers began to arrive, and so did agents from the Federal Bureau of Investigation. The ransom call confirmed that McKay had been kidnapped.

The house was cordoned off with yellow police ribbon, and the corner lot became a crime scene. Neighbors and police officers milled about. Paulette arrived around 11:30 p.m. and was greeted by stares from the people in her yard. She was shocked by the commotion, the squad cars, and the yellow tape strung around the trees, her trees, McKay's trees. What did they know that she didn't? The stares made her sick to her stomach. She immediately sought out Carl, who told her that McKay had been kidnapped. Screaming in agony, she had to be carried into the house.

Inside, the two parents looked into each other's eyes and wondered aloud, "Who would take McKay?" "Why would someone take McKay?" "Where did they take McKay?" So many questions, so many fears, and absolutely no answers forthcoming. The same questions that had been asked by the parents of Bobby Franks, Baby Lindbergh, Bobby Greenlease, and Baby Weinberger. Fear and hysteria gripped these families when their children were grabbed by strangers. Fear and hysteria also gripped the Everetts, who little knew that they had been betrayed by someone close to them.

Chapter 2

Seeds of Betrayal

I was standing there in the execution viewing room and waiting for the curtain to be peeled back when my mind drifted away. I dreamt I was back in Mississippi, and Carl and I were loading our cars. God, it was hot, and we were packing up our things. The cars were stuffed to the ceiling with boxes. We were sweating, but we were happy. We were leaving to find our fortunes, to begin our lives, to do something big. We were together and smiling and laughing. Loading those cars up was fun, and we did not have a care or a worry in the world. God, we were happy. We were going to Texas, we knew the direction, and we just climbed in those cars and took off. We were so young and so full of hope. I was jerked back to reality when the curtain was pulled open and I saw Hilton laid out on the gurney. The I.V. tubes were ready, and Hilton was prepared for his own death. It did not seem real. I had all those good thoughts and then this. I wanted to jump through the window and kill him myself. He made his last statement, I thought of McKay, and then he started turning blue. He was dying right in front of me. I thought, This has to be a dream, it has to be a dream. How did our lives come to this point? How did things get so off track?

The town of Conroe, Texas, is situated in the Piney Woods a few miles north of the sprawling, auto-infested city of Houston. Conroe today is a community of roughly 40,000 people, and like most suburbs it is a nice, quiet place just far enough away from the relentless action of the big city. It did not start out that way. Like many towns in America, Conroe was settled in the late 1800s at the junction of rail lines moving through the area. For decades logging was the main business, but oil was found in the 1930s and changed everything. The oil brought more people, schools, and wealth. Interstate 45 eventually connected Houston and Dallas in the early 1970s, and it brought more cars through Conroe and more people.

The schools are nice in Conroe, as is the downtown area and the lifestyle. One of the main attractions in Conroe is Lake Conroe, a huge freshwater recreational lake northwest of downtown. The lake offers boating, swimming, and great fishing. Many homes in Conroe have two-car garages, one spot for the pickup truck and the other for the high-powered bass boat. The lake's shoreline is also dotted with resorts, golf course communities, and restaurants. Boat tours around the lake with dinner and dancing are available. The entire area suggests a decent life, a good life—nothing over the top, just a pretty good lifestyle.

Like all towns and cities, Conroe has had its share of murder, mayhem, and outrages. In 1937, Bob White, a Montgomery County African-American, was arrested for the rape of a prominent local white landowner's wife. White, who was severely beaten by law enforcement officials, was sentenced to death, but his case was overturned on appeal and he was granted a new trial. After this trial, additional charges of police brutality and prosecutorial misconduct led to a third trial. During jury selection for the third trial, in June of 1941, the victim's husband shot and killed White. The wronged husband was immediately arrested and charged with murder. One week later, he was acquitted.

Clarence Brandley, an African-American, was sentenced to death for the 1980 rape and murder of a young Conroe woman at a local high school. The victim was white. Brandley was granted a stay in 1987, six days before his scheduled execution. Systematic investigation of the case revealed numerous inconsistencies and official misconduct. A new trial was ordered and on January 23, 1990, Brandley was released from death row.

As sensational as these cases were, nothing in its history could prepare Conroe—or even Texas—for the events that took place in September of 1995. Although over 21,000 murders were reported to the police in the U.S. in 1995, the murder that shocked Conroe and nearly brought it to its knees was beyond comprehension. Murder shocks the American conscience, it causes us to stop and ponder, "Why has this happened?" However, the premeditated kidnapping and murder of a child is beyond the pale. The murder of a child cries out for justice. McKay's murder was the culmination of one of history's worse acts of betrayal.

The relationship between the Everetts and the Crawfords began when the Everetts left Mississippi in 1978 to find a better life in Texas. Texas has always been surrounded by a mystique as a big place with big opportunities for big risk-takers. In the 1840s and 1850s revolutionaries, impresarios, assorted hucksters and shysters, crooks on the run, soldiers of fortune, and common hardworking folk flocked to the land beyond the Red River. While different in background and social status, the newcomers were all alike in that they took the risk of coming to Texas to start a new life.

Many a vacant cabin on the frontier had a sign nailed to the front door or on a fence post or gate with the letters *GTT*. Everybody who saw the sign knew that the inhabitants had gone to Texas. Many of these new settlers arrived from other Southern states. Mississippi contributed a large number of new citizens, and these fortune seekers from the Magnolia State sank their roots deep into the Piney Woods of East Texas. Some of the new Texans struck it rich, but many did not. Texas was, and is, a land of wild extremes: desert and swamp, forest and plain, rich and poor, Cadillacs and pickup trucks, tacos and T-bones, boom and bust. The heart and soul of Texas, and Texans, rests on how its people react and adjust to the good times and bad. Opportunity, risk-taking, boom and bust are the characteristics that define the state.

Paulette Everett, the oldest of six children who grew up in Magee, Mississippi, a small town between Jackson and Hattiesburg, was willing to take the risk. Early in her life she dreamed, like many young Mississippians, of leaving the state to have a career and family elsewhere. Mississippi was "too slow," and Paulette wanted adventure and excitement. She was determined not to let the kudzu, a fast-growing jungle vine that envelopes trees and forests in Mississippi, grab her by the feet and hold her down.

Paulette began dating after she graduated from high school.

Her younger sister, Patsy, had a boyfriend named Ricky. One summer, to stay fit for football, Ricky and his friend Carl ran from their hometown of Mendenhall to Magee, a distance of about fifteen miles. While running, the boys would often stop by and visit Patsy. One time the boys came by and were so tired that they camped out in the girls' front yard. Paulette, who was home, met Carl Everett and the two became fast friends, then sweethearts, and, in 1971, husband and wife. They both shared a desire to leave Mississippi, and the key to their escape was education.

In 1977 Paulette and Carl graduated from Mississippi State University. Both earned master's degrees, hers in education and his in forestry. Their degrees were tickets to someplace that promised a better life. Shortly after graduation, Carl was offered jobs in the forest industry, one in Huntsville, Texas, and the other in Rome, Georgia. Like their ancestors before them, the young couple went west, trading the red clay and kudzu of Mississippi for the Piney Woods of East Texas. In the summer of 1978 they loaded their vehicles to the tops of the windows with everything they owned, including one wild cat and two dogs, and drove to Conroe, Texas. The young couple saw that Conroe had two distinct advantages: It was close to the forestry plant for Carl and close to the cultural offerings of Houston for Paulette. Conroe seemed like the perfect fit.

Carl enjoyed his work at the forestry plant, but he disliked snakes. Part of his job called for him to survey forests, and this meant walking around in the woods. The pine forests of East Texas are infested with poisonous snakes, mostly copperheads and coral snakes. Carl wore leggings to protect his limbs from snakebites. A helpful colleague shared with him another piece of forest wisdom: "You better be looking up, too." Snakes liked to curl up around branches and were known to strike people in the neck. Look up, look down—the timber business seemed too dangerous to Carl.

One day in 1979, a friend offered Carl the opportunity to work at Amoco, a Houston-based oil company. The Texas petroleum industry in the late 1970s was in the midst of a real boom, facilitated in part by international events that triggered an explosion in the price of petroleum products. In 1978, the Shah of Iran fled the country, and President Carter decontrolled the price of oil. The price of a barrel of oil was $3.50 in 1972, $9.27 in 1978, and $22.09 in 1980.

By 1983, twenty-eight percent of all Texas tax revenues came from oil and gas operations. The oil industry offered the Everetts a chance to "get in on the action." Texas offered opportunities, but one had to act fast. The pace in Houston was rip-roaring, and Texans were fond of saying, "You better put the pedal to the metal." Carl jumped at the offer and assumed the risk, put down the pedal, and joined the boom.

The Everetts enjoyed the oil and gas industry. Both Carl and Paulette were overwhelmed by the income and prestige that went with the petroleum business in the Houston area. The emphasis was on finding oil to make money to find more oil and to make more money. There seemed to be no end in sight. They purchased a small "3/2" home in Conroe and settled into suburban life. Not bad for a couple of kids from Mississippi.

While Carl was busy finding his rainbow, Paulette did what she had always wanted to do: teach elementary school. She landed a job in New Waverly, a small town just north of Conroe, shortly after they arrived in Texas. In 1980 she transferred to B.B. Rice Elementary School in Conroe. It was nice to teach in the same town where she lived. Paulette, who taught first grade, quickly developed a friendship with the first-grade teacher in the classroom across the hall, Connie Crawford. As teachers they saw each other every day.

Connie and her husband, Hilton, offered their home to the school's faculty and staff for the annual beginning and year-end parties. The Crawford home was located in an upscale subdivision in the southwest area of Conroe. The parties were fun, as the Crawfords liked to entertain and show off their home, a large two-story, well- furnished place, with a huge fenced yard that was nicely landscaped, including an in-ground pool and hot tub. Mounted on the garage facing the driveway was a basketball goal often used for neighborhood games. Hilton was a great host. If he was not cutting-up or telling jokes, he was shooting hoops in the driveway. That Hilton—everybody liked him. He also coached Little League and was good with kids.

Hilton was born March 14, 1939, and grew up in Beaumont, Texas, a blue-collar industrial town tied heavily to the petrochemical business. He graduated from high school in 1955, went to a local college for a few years, and then entered the United States Marine Corps, from which he was discharged in August 1959. Hilton married his high school sweetheart, Connie Parigi, who came from a family that did well in the grocery business. He joined the Beaumont Police Department in 1961. He stayed on the force until 1966, when he took a job at the Jefferson County (Beaumont) Sheriff's Office. After serving as a sheriff's deputy until 1975, he ran for sheriff but lost to the incumbent. Crawford then moved to Conroe, where he began work in the private security business.

Hilton Crawford was essentially two people—not a split personality that turns on and off due to situational factors, but two different people. One Hilton was the family man, the local coach. He was fun to be around. He was jovial and liked to crack jokes—cut up, as Texans say—and keep others in good spirits. He also liked golf. He was a very social individual. Some said he was always happy, always smiling. According to friends, he would do anything for anybody. For years, while his sons, Kevin and Chris, were school-aged, Hilton coached local Little League baseball. He always treated other kids as if they were his own.

As a coach he met two other parents, successful businessmen in the Houston area, and they would play golf together and travel to Las Vegas to gamble. Others in his circle also had money. Hilton's sister was married to a man who owned a number of McDonald's restaurants in southwest Texas. Carl Everett had his own oil and gas company and lived in a large home on a three-acre lot.

If one Hilton Crawford was the jovial family man and Little League coach, the other was the scheming Ralph Kramden, who saw successful business operators all around and wanted a piece of the action for himself. Ralph Kramden, television's lovable "Ralphy Boy," always screwed up the deal, but he always kept his friends. He never hurt anybody but himself.

The Everetts noticed early on that the Crawfords dressed well, wore expensive jewelry, and drove nice cars. This seemed odd because Hilton managed a private security company in Houston and Connie was a schoolteacher, occupations that did not exactly generate vast incomes. The Everetts and the Crawfords occasionally dined together, and it was during one of these dinners that the Crawfords invited

Carl and Paulette to go with them to Las Vegas. Hilton did the same thing with his other friends, and it was not unusual for Connie to invite couples from school to Las Vegas. The Crawfords went to Vegas two or three times a year, and their guests only had to pay for airfare. Hilton had connections in the hotels and got the complimentary rooms. Paulette declined, but Carl eventually accompanied Hilton on gambling trips to Las Vegas and Atlantic City. Hilton seemed like a high roller.

The Crawfords liked to talk about their gambling trips and the money they won in Vegas and New Jersey. Once the Everetts were in the Crawfords' home visiting at the breakfast table when Hilton got up, left the room, and returned with a large shoebox. He was really excited and said he was going to show the Everetts more money than they had ever seen at one time. Like a kid with a Christmas present, he removed the lid and revealed a box filled with cash of varying denominations. Shocked, the Everetts asked Hilton why he kept the money at home and not in a bank. He laughed and said he was really good at gambling.

After several trips with Hilton to Atlantic City, Carl told Paulette that he was uncomfortable about Hilton's behavior and gambling associates. But while the joint gambling excursions ended, the friendship between Carl and Hilton continued and even deepened.

Hilton had nice clothes, a nice house with a swimming pool, jewelry, and an upscale lifestyle that suggested wealth. He "played the ponies" and gambled excessively in Las Vegas and Atlantic City. One close friend stated that Hilton was addicted to and consumed by gambling and said he "would bet on anything."

On March 1, 1983, Samuel McKay Everett was born. He was an alert baby with uncommonly blue eyes and beautiful features. He was active and constantly on the move. He climbed on everything and seemed to walk earlier than most children. The boy was bright and full of promise. Once he learned to walk he began riding toys and soon was pedaling his own bicycle. He loved skateboarding, rollerblading, and swimming. McKay was also intuitive and sensitive. Because he was an only child, he grew up with adults, was accustomed to interacting with them, and felt secure around them. Like most children, McKay was also told to beware of strangers.

For the Everetts, life was very good. Carl and Paulette began their own oil and gas company. Paulette left teaching to manage the company office. They fell into the rhythm of parenthood and work. Connie and Hilton Crawford continued to invite the Everetts to the school parties and to dinner every now and then. The Everetts sold their starter home and began building their dream home. They rented a house in the same subdivision as the Crawfords, and McKay rode his bike and played with the Crawford boys, Chris and Kevin.

In 1990 the Everetts moved into a new neighborhood in northwest Conroe, a fifteen-minute drive from downtown. Their new home was a two-story 6,500-square-foot brick home that occupied three acres along a corner lot. Over 500 azaleas and assorted bushes adorned the yard. The narrow driveway from the street to the back door of the house and garage area faced north and was heavily wooded with pine and oak trees. It was roughly fifty to sixty yards from the street to the back door. The driveway, with its length and abundant tree cover, suggested seclusion and privacy. The street that intersected the Everetts' driveway was narrow, about twelve-feet wide. Vehicles backing down the driveway had to be careful not to back up too far on the street or else they would end up in the ditch or hit the neighbor's mailbox.

There were children for McKay to play with in this new neighborhood. The dense woods that divided the neighboring houses was no obstacle to the children. The forests and empty lots had paths cut through where the children would walk to each other's houses. The kids even built crosswalks and little bridges over the brooks and streams in the woods. Traffic in the area was minimal, and when the kids were not in the woods they were riding bikes up and down the streets. On the 4th of July the neighbors cooked out together, and on Halloween the adults organized games for the kids. There was a sense of neighborhood here, a sense of calm, a belief that kids were always safe.

Even though McKay developed new friendships in his new neighborhood, the Everetts never forgot about their old friends. They carried McKay over to the Crawfords' home on Halloween, where the old friends stuffed his "trick-or-treat" bag with candy. The Crawfords remembered McKay on special occasions and always gave him Christmas gifts.

As McKay grew older, he would return to the Crawfords' house and swim in their pool. He learned how to play video games on Kevin's computer. McKay became attached to Hilton and Connie Crawford to such an extent that he began to call them "Uncle Hilty" and "Aunt Connie." To McKay, the Crawfords were more than friends, more than neighbors—they were family. McKay had real blood aunts and uncles, but most of them lived in Mississippi. The Crawfords, however, were nearby and there was no harm in calling family friends *uncle* and *aunt*.

Carl and Hilton eventually did what many people advise friends not to do—they entered into business ventures together. Hilton was fascinated with money and the things that money could buy, like cars, homes, jewelry, and trips to Atlantic City. Sometime around 1985, Carl sold Hilton and one of his friends an interest in an oil and gas well. Investing in this oil well was a high-risk venture, and the results of the investments were not good. The well was—as they say in the oil business—a dry hole, and they ended up losing nearly $10,000. All three lost their investments.

Hilton later offered Carl an opportunity to participate in a restaurant venture. However, before he could become a partner in the Conroe eatery, Hilton informed Carl that he needed a copy of the Everetts' financial statements. Carl forwarded this information to Hilton, but the Everetts' attorney advised him not to become involved in Hilton Crawford's restaurant venture. At the time, the Everetts were worth several million dollars in cash, stocks, and mutual funds, and property. Indeed, the kids from Mississippi had done well. The Texas oil boom had changed their lives. Carl decided against joining in on the restaurant enterprise, which eventually went under. Carl had become involved enough, though, that Hilton became well aware of the Everetts' financial situation.

In the late 1980s the oil and gas industry began to slow. The boom was over, and it was time to move into other areas for family income. In early 1993, the Everetts' neighbor asked them to consider Amway. The possibility of quick additional money seemed intriguing, and Carl Everett soon worked the Amway circuit during his spare time. Hilton and Connie Crawford followed suit and got involved in the business.

In February 1995, Carl asked Paulette to host a make-up party in the home of an Amway member. Paulette called a number of friends, including Connie Crawford, and invited them to attend the party. When Paulette called the Crawfords, Hilton answered the phone. The Everetts knew that Hilton placed his bets, typically on horses and ballgames, via the phone. Paulette said, "I hope I am not interrupting some important conversation."

Hilton replied in a serious voice, "I don't do that [gambling] anymore, it's bad for my health." Paulette hung up the phone and told Carl that Hilton sounded as if he must have been in some trouble over his gambling. She advised Carl to avoid him.

Unknown to the Everetts and even to his own family was the fact that Hilton was not only in trouble—he was in very *serious* trouble. By 1995, he owed hundreds of thousands of dollars to local bookies in and around Houston. The bookies were also squeezing Hilton to pay up or face the consequences. Hilton had an unshareable problem—he could not tell anyone about his debts. He was desperate to find a way out.

Paulette attended the make-up party, and she noticed that Connie Crawford seemed uncomfortable there. Other women were eagerly buying make-up and other personal items, but Connie bought nothing. While it was not uncommon for participants not to purchase anything, it seemed odd that Connie Crawford went home without so much a single a tube of lipstick.

It was late August of 1995, and McKay was planning on playing football in the upcoming school year. Carl and McKay went over to the Crawfords' house and McKay played basketball with Hilton in the driveway. They also tossed around a football. The garage door was up, and Carl glanced at the gold car inside, noting a fancy emblem on the rear. A second later they were back to playing basketball, but the image of the emblem was permanently stored in his brain. Weeks later the significance of this image would become clear.

In September of 1995, McKay had just started seventh grade at Peet Junior High in Conroe. An Amway meeting was scheduled for 8:00 p.m. on the 12th, and the Everetts made plans to attend the get-together. Hilton Crawford called the Everetts sometime around September 3 to see if they were going to the meeting; they told Hilton that they were. Hilton called again on the 12th around 4:30 p.m. to verify the Everetts' plans. Nothing had changed. Since the meeting was on a school night, McKay would stay home and finish his homework. It was not unusual for the Everetts to leave McKay at home alone for short periods—the house had a security system, and the neighborhood was a safe place.

Chapter 3

The Week from Hell

I'll never forget that week as long as I live. It started out normal and ended up with my son murdered and his body found in a swamp. Nobody can understand it or even comprehend what happened. It still seems unreal to me today, like a dream, like it never happened. It was a nightmare. One day I was talking to and laughing with McKay and helping him with his homework, and the next day he was gone. Life is so precious because you never know when it can be taken away. I remember so well watching him out on the football field. I was so proud of McKay. He was just finding his wings—the whole world was open to him. He was ready to start participating in other things that were different. He was having fun. And then, boom, just like that it was over. It makes no sense at all. It still seems unreal. God made the world in seven days. Seven days to make this world. Seven days to make something good. It took a week to make the world, and it took a week to destroy my world. I try to explain this to other people, to try to help them understand my reality, but nobody understands. One week I was reading with my son, and then I was forced to make plans to bury my son. A week sounds like nothing, but it's enough to change a life forever. I know because it happened to me.

Monday, September 11, 1995, was a typical morning in the Everett household. Carl and Paulette awoke around 6:30. McKay usually awoke around 6:45. Paulette prepared breakfast, and together the three ate and then readied themselves for the day. McKay's favorite food was grits, and sometimes the Everetts would have grit-spitting contests. But this day, the excitement around the table focused on football, a time-honored Texas tradition. It is in seventh grade that most Texas schoolboys begin their football careers. This was a time to talk about positions, plays, games, and the excitement leading up to the game. McKay was going to play in his first football game after school. He was not very athletic, but he was willing to try, and that is what counted in football—it was worth the risk. Carl was very proud of his son.

Just before Carl took McKay to school that morning, he snapped a picture of the budding footballer with his overstuffed backpack and broad grin, heavy with braces and rubber bands. Later that day, as usual, Paulette picked McKay up from school. When they got home, he finished his homework, snacked on yogurt, and daydreamed about the upcoming game. They had dinner with Paulette's mother, who was in town helping with Paulette's brother's new baby. The football game that evening was uneventful, and it was hard to tell who won or lost. The field was mass chaos with players and coaches running everywhere. The players all looked the same in their uniforms and pads, but McKay was spotted running to the huddle for one play, and the play was over in twenty seconds. It did not matter how long he played, just as long as he played. McKay was proud. It was a wonderful day, a special day.

On Tuesday, September 12, 1995, the Everett household came to life in the same order as it always had. The family downed breakfast, and Carl and McKay left for school. As he was getting out of the car at school, McKay looked at Carl and said, "How 'bout those Lions?" which was code for *I love you*. McKay, like most teenagers, especially boys, shied away from open displays of affection. On this day, for some reason, he did not.

As usual, Paulette picked McKay up from school, and they went out for yogurt, after which he did his homework. Routines were good things. On this day he had a fun homework assignment—he had to write a paper on how someone would spend a million dollars. McKay dictated while Paulette typed his answer. Mom and son laughed at the spending plan and joked about how homework can, on some occasions, be a fun thing to do.

Carl and Paulette had the Amway meeting at 8:00 p.m., and McKay was in no mood for a sitter. After all, he was twelve, independent, and like most youngsters, he thought he could take care of himself. Besides, the Amway meeting was close, and the house had an alarm. The neighborhood was a quiet place where nothing ever happened.

Crawford called the Everetts around 4:30 p.m. to make sure there were no changes in the plans. Around 5 p.m. Hilton and Connie drove over to her sister Anna Marie Mazzu's house for supper. The Crawfords left the Mazzu residence around 6:30 p.m. The couple came and left together in the same vehicle.

Carl was in Houston on business, and he was going to meet Paulette at the Amway gathering. Paulette and Randy Bartlett, a neighbor and family friend, would come to the meeting together. The Amway get-together took place in a high-rise building in downtown Conroe a few steps away from the Montgomery County Courthouse. The exact distance between the Everett home and the meeting place was six miles, or ten minutes, depending on lights and traffic.

As Paulette and Randy were preparing to leave, McKay was sitting in a chair in the den eating ice cream from the carton. It was overcast and a light drizzle had fallen. Paulette instructed McKay to keep the phone ready to call the neighbors should the weather turn nasty. She set out a flashlight in case the lights failed. As in most households with kids, contingency plans were always needed, not for the kids but for the peace of mind of the parents.

McKay turned on the alarm system as Paulette and Randy left the house around 8:00 p.m. He had been taught how to arm and disarm the alarm system and actually knew more about the alarm than did Carl or Paulette. McKay had also been taught not to open the door for strangers—or anyone, for that matter. McKay would never open the door for a stranger.

Paulette and Randy arrived at the Amway meeting around 8:15 p.m. and met up with Carl. The rain had begun. Paulette remarked to Randy about being uneasy with McKay home alone. Randy offered calm assurances. Paulette sat by a window and listened, but not to the people at the meeting. Business was being conducted, but she was not taking any notice of the discussion. Actually, Paulette was daydreaming, and at one point she looked out the window through the rain and saw a car drive past. She wondered where the car might be going on a night like this.

The meeting adjourned around 10:00 p.m. The Everetts and several others decided to get a cup of coffee at a nearby restaurant. About eight people made it to the coffee shop, found a table, and ordered refreshments. The group made small talk. At one point, Carl got up from the table and called home from a pay phone; McKay still had not answered the phone. Carl told Paulette about the phone call and informed the group he was going home. He left the restaurant and drove the short distance home. It took him approximately ten minutes to get to the house.

Later on, Randy left the table, returned, and told Paulette that he was ready to leave. They said goodbye to the others at the table. As they were leaving the coffee shop parking lot around 11:00 p.m., Randy informed Paulette that he had just spoken with Carl, who said McKay was not at home and could not be found. Carl also told Randy that when he arrived at home he noticed that the back door was ajar and that the alarm had been turned off. Worse, the house was absolutely silent. Even though McKay was an only child, he was a teenager, and the television was usually on and the phone would ring constantly. A silent house was an omen. Upon hearing this news Paulette, who feared the worst, screamed and screamed, crouched in the front seat and then balled up on the floorboard. It was a guttural scream, one that made fear and terror come alive in the car.

Carl searched the house for McKay. Sometime between 11 and 11:15 p.m. the phone rang and Carl lifted the receiver. Maybe it was McKay. Instead, a raspy female voice on the other end asked, "Who is this?"

Carl answered, "This is Carl Everett."

The caller said, "We have your son. We got him." The caller also demanded a $500,000 ransom, and the money was to be in $100 bills. Carl was told that they would call back on Wednesday (September 13) at 8:00 a.m. with more instructions and information about where to find McKay.

Carl called 911 to alert the local authorities and the FBI. It seemed as if it took forever for the police to arrive. The ransom call erased all doubt that McKay was simply missing or had run off with friends, but Carl could not accept the fact that McKay had actually been kidnapped.

When Paulette and Randy arrived at the Everett residence, they found a number of people in the front yard. Paulette immediately searched the crowd to find Carl. One of Carl's friends grabbed her by the shoulders as she screamed, "Where is my baby?" He said no one knew, but his face hinted at fear and horror. Her screaming continued for several minutes and then ceased.

"That's it!" Paulette told herself, "McKay is out joyriding with one of the neighbor kids who's old enough to drive." This was a reasonable explanation. It was not only possible—it was probable. Her heart told her that everything was okay. Mothers always think about good endings. Everything was going to be okay.

A split second later her mind brought reality home. Paulette knew that McKay, though a full-fledged teenager, was not devious or underhanded. He knew and understood the rules. He always told his parents where he was going and with whom. He was not the kind of kid who would impulsively run out of the house and not tell anyone where he was going. Her mind sifted through everything that was happening and reached a different conclusion. Despite the chaos and emotionalism unfolding around her, Paulette's mind told her that McKay was not out with friends—someone had taken him from the house. Paulette went into the house and sank down in a rocking chair in the kitchen.

Carl phoned the Crawford residence—he needed help, and he needed his friend, Hilton. He made the call around 11:40 p.m. He thought that Hilton, with his law enforcement and security business background, would know what to do. Hilton would know whom to call and how to get things organized. Carl informed Connie Crawford about McKay's disappearance and asked to speak to Hilton. But Hilton was not home. Carl asked her for Hilton's mobile number and his whereabouts—everyone was needed to help find McKay. Connie replied that she did not know where Hilton was, nor did she know Hilton's mobile phone number.

Paulette was taken to the home of the Kahns, neighbors who lived across the street. Bill Kahn had reported that while he was taking out the trash in the early evening, he had seen a gold, late-model Chrysler back out of the Everett residence. The neighbor also reported that the car had nearly hit the trash can that he had placed on the grass near the street. As the car sped away, the neighbor noted that the vehicle was a four-door and had an emblem that read *Crown*

Motors on the left rear of the trunk. This information later proved to be the "clincher" as the investigation progressed. Though Kahn got a good look at the car's exterior, the windows were deeply tinted, offering no glimpse of the car's interior or the occupants. He was not able to see who was driving or who was inside.

Around 11:30 p.m., Paulette made the short walk home from the Kahns. Her feet felt like two concrete blocks. The unfolding situation, like a ton of bricks that had suddenly fallen from the sky, landed squarely on her shoulders and drove her feet into the yard. As she walked onto her property and passed the trees that she and McKay had planted together, she was greeted by the yellow strips of police tape all along the driveway. Nearing the back door, she could see fingerprint dust. Opening the door revealed a number of people in FBI jackets dusting the furniture and other places where a fingerprint might be found. It was not her house anymore. In the span of a few hours it had changed from a home to a crime scene. The place resembled a movie set, with one exception: It was real, and there were no actors at 5438 Pine Springs Court Road.

The much-anticipated call from the kidnappers with instructions about where to leave the ransom money and where to find McKay never materialized. Why didn't they call? After the failed telephone call, the FBI proceeded to another level of investigation. The investigators immediately took charge and told Carl and Paulette that they had tapped the phones to prepare for additional kidnapper calls and ransom demands. The FBI also asked the Everetts to prepare three lists, one for trust, one for love, and one for respect. They were instructed to put the names of people McKay trusted, loved, and respected, including his parents, on the lists. Who would McKay open the door for? Everyone they knew was a potential suspect.

As the Everetts completed the lists, they realized that whoever had taken McKay would not have been at the Amway meeting, would have had a key to their house, would have known about the alarm system, or would have known the family schedule. Whoever took McKay also had to have known him and his habits very well. He would not have gone anywhere with a stranger. The house had not been broken into or ransacked. The back door had not been kicked in or damaged. The reality was that McKay had left willingly with someone. It had to be someone he knew. The Everetts also realized as they were forming their lists that they were naming potential suspects, and that thought was chilling. How could a friend do this? They quickly forgot about their personal feelings and got down to doing what the FBI had requested. Their child was missing, and this was no time for sentimentalities. The minutes were ticking away and every second was precious. If they were to find McKay alive, they had to act fast.

Once the fingerprinting operation concluded, the FBI turned the Everett home into a command center. Carl and Paulette assumed the role of guests. Carl's office became the site for private meetings, another upstairs room was turned into the polygraph center, and the kitchen area became the receiving and holding room where countless numbers of people came and went, visited with the Everetts, talked to the investigators, or left food. The bathroom was the only private area where the Everetts could talk or escape from the commotion.

As Carl showered on the morning of the 13th, he remembered something—his mind pulled up an image he had seen before. It was the emblem Bill Kahn reported seeing on the car that backed out of the Everett residence on September 12. Carl told Paulette that he, too, had seen the same emblem. He remembered seeing it three weeks earlier when he and McKay were at the Crawford place playing basketball in the driveway. Hilton and McKay were shooting hoops and laughing it up. The garage door was up, and Carl noticed the emblem on Hilton's gold car. His mind had snapped a picture of the emblem and then stored it for later use. He got dressed and told the FBI about the emblem.

Who committed this crime? Was someone in the neighborhood involved? The investigators had a lot of questions that needed to be answered, and everyone was a suspect. Yet the investigators had to weed out some of the potential suspects because time was of the essence. They decided to use the polygraph machine to narrow the field of possible suspects.

Polygraph tests measure certain physiological characteristics, like a person's heart rate, breathing rate, and blood pressure. The theory underlying a polygraph test is that lying induces stress, and that stress can be measured and recorded on a machine for additional analysis. Polygraphs also measure tiny changes in the electrical conductivity of the skin caused by sweating. Liars sweat. Lie detectors monitor these functions, and the examiner can show at what point during the questioning period changes in the various biological reactions to questions occur. If the period of greatest biological reaction lines up with the key questions on the graph paper, stress is alleged. The assumption of stress indicates lies, which suggest, in criminal cases, personal involvement. Results from polygraph tests are not admissible in court. However, in cases like McKay's abduction, law enforcement personnel employ the polygraph or machine to eliminate suspects.

Carl Everett was first up for the polygraph. When he was approached to submit to a polygraph test, he laughed, mocking the usefulness of such a device. This was a kidnapping, not an ugly divorce case filled with affairs and lunchtime hotel sessions. A demonstration was needed, and Carl was hooked up to the machine. The first question was, "Have you ever lied to Mrs. Everett?" to which Carl replied, "No." The operator noted the untruthfulness of the answer detected by the machine. The demonstration concluded, the only humorous moment in an otherwise horrific ordeal. Carl was questioned and then eliminated as a suspect. The experience was bitter, but necessary.

The next person to be polygraphed was Ric Metts, a family friend. The Everetts first met Ric in 1983 at the First Baptist Church in Conroe. He was single, in his early thirties, and lived with his mother and father. Ric, like the Everetts, loved animals, especially dogs, and he would come over to the Everetts' house and watch their three dogs and three cats when they left town. The Everetts trusted Ric, and he always left the house and animals in good shape. Ric and McKay had grown into a relationship that resembled that of brothers, one minute laughing and talking and the next minute arguing. Ric also babysat McKay when Carl and Paulette went out. He had a key to the Everett residence, and his name figured prominently on the three lists. He was also someone whom McKay would open the door for.

The FBI investigators thought Ric fit the profile of someone who might abuse a young person. After all, Ric was in his thirties, single, and still living at home with his mother and father. He was definitely a suspect. More to the point, Carl Everett informed the

FBI that the ransom caller had a gravelly voice, and Ric's sister had a gravelly voice. Armed with this information, the FBI immediately contacted Ric at work.

Metts answered the phone around 11 a.m. on September 13—it was the librarian from the school that McKay attended. She asked Ric if he had heard about McKay. Ric said that he had not, and the caller informed him that McKay was missing and had probably been kidnapped. He hung up the phone and drove straight to the Everett residence. He found the house in disarray, with police and FBI agents everywhere. Ric found Paulette lying on a couch. She was lethargic, yet her facial expression was one of pure panic.

Ric felt the stares of the FBI agents. As he was leaving the house to return to work, they asked him a few questions about his relationship with the Everetts and with McKay. Ric returned to work, where a short time later seven FBI agents interviewed him. He also gave the FBI permission to search his residence, and six agents scoured his home.

He agreed to submit to a polygraph test. After work he went to the FBI office in The Woodlands. The polygraph exam lasted an hour, and he was cleared. At the time Metts was very disappointed at being treated or perceived as a suspect. He had heard statements like, "Just tell us what you did with him and this will all end." Ric had been terrified, but at the same time he realized that time was of the essence and that the agents were just trying to find McKay. "They were only doing their job," he said. Most of all he ached at what the Everetts were going through.

Paulette Everett was not polygraphed. Her emotional condition prevented any meaningful interview by the FBI. And her body followed her emotional condition. In the early morning hours of September 13, Paulette experienced a jolt that raised her off the sofa on which she was lying, and her left arm began to pull up toward her body. It would not straighten out. Something was terribly wrong.

It was now Thursday, September 14, and McKay had been missing for three days. No more ransom calls had come, and the tension was mounting. The FBI officials requested that the Everetts not go public with the news of McKay's abduction and ransom out of fear for McKay's well-being. They agreed, and the hours rolled by. The media began to descend on the once quiet neighborhood. The yellow tape around the yard was news that something was wrong. A joint afternoon news conference was called by the FBI and the Montgomery County Sheriff's Department to release the first official details of McKay's abduction.

The same afternoon Hilton Crawford gave written consent to the FBI to impound and search his gold 1994 Chrysler. When the agents opened the trunk, they noticed the lining had recently been removed. The agents also noticed that the dealership emblem on the Chrysler's trunk had been removed. Crawford told the FBI agents that he left Conroe on September 12 at 8:10 p.m. and went to Lufkin, Texas, to meet Karen, an employee of Security Guard Services, the company he worked for. Crawford then stated that he left Lufkin around 9:30 p.m. and proceeded to Jasper, Texas. He further stated that he left Jasper around 11:30 p.m. and drove to Beaumont, Texas, arriving there around 1:00 a.m. He checked into a Best Western Motel at 1:30 a.m. Hilton the family friend was slowly transforming into Hilton the prime suspect.

Paulette Everett withdrew into herself. Her body and speech pattern became slower and slower. She remained hopeful and imagined that McKay would just walk up to the house or jump out of someone's car and run into the house. She dreamed, like any parent, like any mother, of a happy ending. The entire scene was otherworldly.

The FBI began to narrow their focus by using the three lists and the description of the gold car and watching who came and went from the Everett residence. They told the Everetts that they wanted to question Hilton Crawford, but that Crawford had refused to submit to a polygraph test because of "high blood pressure." It was clear that he was nervous.

As the investigation proceeded, the Everett household was besieged with visitors dropping by to express concern. One such visitor was Jeremy, who worked at a local car dealership. As he was standing in the kitchen talking with the Everetts, he told them that Crawford had recently ordered a new mat for his trunk. The Everetts told him to provide the FBI with this information. The pieces of the puzzle were slowly falling into place. Hilton was now a prime suspect.

The police investigators learned that Hilton Crawford owned

a gold-colored car, the same type of vehicle that Bill Kahn had seen backing out of the Everetts' residence on the evening of September 12. Most important, the investigators knew that Hilton Crawford's name figured prominently in the lists assembled by the Everetts. Hilton was a person that McKay trusted and loved. Carl and Paulette believed that McKay would open the door if Hilton asked McKay to do so and probably even go with him if he gave the boy a good reason.

The FBI investigated Hilton's whereabouts on September 12. They also analyzed his cell phone records and found that Crawford had recently contacted several employees of the security company he managed. These employees were interviewed, and the FBI found out that Hilton had tried to enlist these employees' help in fabricating an alibi. Additional analysis of the phone records revealed that one person, Irene Flores, age 55, was contacted by Crawford six times on the night of September 12. Hilton called Flores at 7:55 p.m., and the call lasted one minute and fifteen seconds; the second call was at 8:11 p.m. and lasted twenty-eight seconds; and the third call was at 8:37 p.m. and lasted two minutes and twenty-nine seconds. Hilton made a two-minute call to Flores from Lake Charles, Louisiana, at 11:10 p.m.; there was a second call, lasting three minutes, at 11:13 p.m.; he made a third and final call to Flores at 11:30 p.m., and it lasted six minutes.

Flores was interviewed and arrested, and eventually she confessed to making the ransom call. In a written statement made to law enforcement authorities, Flores stated that she had known Hilton for about ten years and had even worked for Crawford for several years in the late 1980s. She stated that Crawford called her at work—she worked for the Harris County (Houston) Parks and Recreation Department—in early September and asked her if she wanted to make some money. Crawford told her that all she had to do was make one phone call and she would make $30,000. All she had to do was call Mr. Everett, say that McKay had been abducted, and ask for money. Crawford instructed her to ask for $500,000 in $100 bills in bundles of $10,000. She stated that Crawford told her to use a pay phone anywhere to call Mr. Everett. A friend drove her to a pay phone, and she called the Everett residence about thirty or forty times until Mr. Everett finally answered the phone. She said she told him everything as instructed. She also stated that Mr. Everett told her that if he could not speak to his son there was no deal and he hung up. Flores stated that after the telephone call she went directly home and straight to bed.

The information gleaned from Irene Flores was critical in narrowing the list of suspects and the entire investigation to Hilton Crawford. The floodlights on Hilton narrowed to a single beam when investigators learned that he had called the Everetts' home several times to determine their plans to attend the last two Amway meetings. Hilton was now the prime suspect in the kidnapping, and the circle was closing.

On Friday, September 15, at 7:00 a.m., Hilton Crawford, age 56, was arrested at his home in the Rivershire subdivision of Conroe. At 1:30 p.m., he was officially charged with aggravated kidnapping. The news media reported to the public that McKay had been kidnapped, and Conroe, the quiet Houston suburb, was rocked with a major news story that took off across the state and the nation. The media coverage was intense, and trucks of various TV stations were parked up and down the street near the Everett home. The serene suburban neighborhood was now a crime scene. The news media wanted answers, but the only case information available was the ransom call, the lists assembled by the Everetts, and the description of the gold car. Carl Everett became incensed at the media as it was reported that he was not McKay's real father. How this false information surfaced was never established.

Hilton was in jail, but McKay was still missing. The investigators and the Everetts believed that he was still alive. While in his jail cell, Hilton thanked a jailer for treating him in a respectful manner. The jailer noted that Crawford had tears in his eyes. Crawford asked him if he could place a phone call to his wife because he had made a bad mistake and needed to talk to her. Crawford repeated, "I've made a bad mistake. I told Remington to put the kid on a bus. I hope he's all right. I've made a bad mistake." It seemed as if to Hilton McKay was on a field trip, an adventure.

The authorities allowed Hilton to place the call. Crawford also stated to the jailer, "The FBI asked me a lot of things. My mind has been a little clouded. I'm remembering more now. I took the boy to Lafayette, Louisiana. Remington met me there. He was in a '93 or '94 burgundy-colored Cadillac. Remington took the boy to New Orleans. If the deal worked out or anything went wrong, Remington was supposed to put the boy on the bus today or tomorrow and send him home." The jailer forwarded this information to his supervisors. This information fueled the belief that McKay was still alive.

On Saturday, September 16, Carl Everett asked Paulette to go to Connie Crawford and ask her to go to the jail and get Hilton to draw a map showing the whereabouts of McKay. Paulette dressed and had a neighbor drive her to the home of Connie's sister, Ann Marie Mazzu, in Willis, where Connie was staying. When Connie heard that Paulette was outside standing in the driveway, she ran out of the house and down the driveway screaming.

At this point, Connie became hysterical and kept screaming, "McKay's dead! McKay's dead! I know he's dead! Hilton hired a hit man! They found the car mats, they found the bloody car mats." Connie also wondered out loud why Hilton had not just killed himself.

They went into Ann Marie's house, and Connie continued to scream, "McKay's dead! McKay's dead! I know he's dead. Oh, my God, oh, my God!" It was a frightening scene. How did she know McKay was dead?

Connie then sat down and started talking about Hilton, their financial difficulties, and his gambling problem. She spoke frantically about a shipping business venture involving chickens in which they had invested. A load of chickens had been shipped to Houston, but the U.S. Customs officials had refused to allow the freight into the country and the chickens had spoiled. For a guy in the private security business, investing in chickens seemed odd and very risky. It was a long shot for a little guy. What happened? Where did everything go wrong?

Paulette broke in and asked Connie to take her son Kevin with her and go to the jail and ask Hilton to draw a map so the authorities could locate McKay. She then returned home. A news conference was scheduled for 12:30 p.m. on the lawn of the Everett residence. A television set was placed near Hilton's jail cell so he could watch and hear the Everetts plea for McKay.

Carl held a football and spoke into the camera, addressing Hilton:

"I just want you to search down real deep in your heart. Whatever did happen, I hope your heart will just soften and understand that all we really want is for McKay to be back home and safe. In my heart I know that you would never harm my son. You loved him like your own son. You gave him this ball. He called you Uncle Hilty, and he loved you dearly. Three weeks ago, we were at your home playing with this ball, and when we got ready to leave, I said, 'Go give Uncle Hilty a hug,' and McKay came over and hugged you and kissed you on your forehead."

Perhaps moved by Carl's emotional plea, Hilton drew a map that led authorities to McKay. The child's decomposing body was discovered on September 17, near Interstate 10, some fifteen miles from Lafayette, Louisiana. The place, called Whiskey Bay, is a huge swamp in Iberville Parish. Whiskey Bay is, as the caption says on Louisiana's car tags, "A Sportsman's Paradise." Alternatively, Whiskey Bay is also a murderer's paradise because it is a large swamp, a perfect place to dispose of bodies—it is a boneyard. With the discovery of McKay's body in that place, the Everetts' worst nightmare became reality. Their son was dead, betrayed and murdered by a family friend.

The autopsy on McKay remains concluded that he had been severely beaten on the head, possibly with a metal flashlight, and shot at least twice with a .45 caliber handgun. Hilton confessed to the kidnapping and even to being present at McKay's killing. However, he blamed the murder on an associate named R.L. Remington. Further investigation into the crime recovered the gun, the trunk lining from Hilton's car, and clothes that Crawford had cleaned at a local dry cleaners right after the killing. The owner of the dry cleaners said that the clothes were stained even after being dry-cleaned.

On September 20, 1995, Crawford agreed to take a polygraph test. He answered "Yes" to five specific questions:

—Were you present at the very time that McKay was shot at Whiskey Bay?

—Was McKay actually killed at Whiskey Bay like you said?

—Was your Smith & Wesson .45 the only gun used to shoot McKay?

—Did you really see the man you call R.L. Remington shoot McKay exactly like you said?

—Were there really four people present that you claim at the Whiskey Bay site when McKay was shot?

The polygraph operator noted consistent deception by Hilton in questions four and five. Prior to the exam, Crawford admitted that he had kidnapped McKay, but he refused to answer direct questions as to whether or not he had shot and killed McKay.

A Montgomery County grand jury reviewed the assembled evidence and on September 20 indicted Hilton Crawford for capital murder. A capital indictment put Crawford in serious trouble because in 1995 Texas was the nation's leader in executions. Between 1982 and 1994, the state had executed 85 capital offenders. In 1995 it put 19 more to death. Execution in Texas was more than a possibility—it was probable. Texas was a place that did not put up with cold-blooded murder, and it was a state that had little time for people who killed kids.

Stripped of nice clothes and a suburban lifestyle and confined in a tiny cell, Hilton had hit rock bottom. Ever the gambler, he was not ready to fold his hand. The trial that awaited him represented his last chance to tell his side of the story. He wanted to tell people that he did not kill McKay. Sure, he assisted in the kidnapping; sure, he planned the crime; sure, he tried to fake an alibi. But he was no murderer. He was once a coach, and coaches do not kill children.

About six weeks after McKay's body was discovered in the Louisiana Swamp and analyzed by forensic experts, his remains were returned to the Everetts. Carl made the arrangements for the funeral. The Everetts felt cheated and felt as if their friends and family had been denied the opportunity to say good-bye to McKay. The time between the discovery and return of the body had not removed or diminished the sense of loss.

Carl visited with the local funeral home and requested that he and Paulette have some time alone with McKay before the burial. The room where the boy's remains lay had no flowers. His casket was blue and had an Elvis Presley blanket draped across the top. Carl took the time to spray McKay's cologne on the blanket. The scent prompted numerous thoughts and emotions in Carl and Paulette. Paulette could not talk, but she calmly stroked the coffin. She could think only of holding McKay. She was amazed at Carl's courage and resolve in attending to the details of the funeral.

Music began to play. It was so soft that Paulette thought she was imagining things. These were the songs that she had played for McKay at night. The songs were played over and over, in the same order. Carl asked someone for a magic marker. He removed the blanket and began to write on the coffin. Then Paulette wrote, *Thank you for gracing my life. I miss the grit fights.* This is how the Everetts spent their final private moments with McKay. And then it was over.

At the gravesite, one of the FBI agents who had assisted in the investigation came dressed in a traditional Scottish kilt and played "Amazing Grace" on the bagpipes. The echo of the notes floated through the air and through those at the gravesite. At the conclusion of the service, Paulette returned to their vehicle. Carl remained at the gravesite. He stood and sobbed and talked to McKay and apologized for not seeing the real Hilton Crawford. His shoulders heaved with each apology.

Little did the Everetts know that a portion of McKay's remains were not buried. A tuft of McKay's hair, some teeth, and some bone fragments were later found and returned to the Everetts. These remains were cremated.

Chapter 4

Delaying the Inevitable

I did not know what to expect as the prosecutor geared up for the trial. You know, we were not informed of anything, and Carl and I thought that once Hilton was indicted for capital murder, the trial would start right away. I had no sense of how the criminal justice system works. We were right in the middle of things, and we did not know anything. That is how things work. I have watched television shows and movies about crime, and the only vision or knowledge I had about the criminal justice system came from these shows. I had to rely on the district attorney's office to keep me informed, and they were usually busy. I had no idea that Hilton would sit in jail for almost a year before his actual trial. Everything just took so long to occur. It was depressing. It was tough, real tough, to go on living with my grief, knowing Hilton was sitting in jail and watching television, trying to figure out a way to get off. This just killed me.

Runnymede is a meadow along the Thames River west of London. It's quiet today, except for the occasional tourist or local walking a dog. Runnymede, however, is not just another ordinary park. This place is hallowed ground, and in 1995 Hilton Crawford was a benefactor of the events that took place there in 1215.

In that year, King John signed the Magna Carta, a document that is today the cornerstone of our civil liberties, which protects individuals against the unjust and arbitrary decisions of any ruler. In 1215, English barons, tired of high taxes and the ruthless and brutal persecution of those who refused to pay, took up arms against King John and captured London. In return for peace, they demanded from the King a charter of liberties to protect individuals against the naked power of the Crown. Negotiations held at Runnymede led to the Magna Carta, or Great Charter.

One of the rights set out in the Magna Carta was the right to a speedy trial. Crawford's plight was far away from Runnymede in geography and time. Indeed, his case arose 780 years after the barons negotiated a deal with the King. He was no baron standing up for his rights against the whims of the government. However, Crawford was going to take full advantage of rights and benefits that had their origins in feudal England. It was his right to *exercise* his rights, and his lawyers were well prepared to use the system for their client's benefit.

Americans have numerous rights, and at the slightest insult or injury, some are quick to tell friends, enemies, and strangers, "I got rights." But many take these rights, real and perceived, for granted. Ask any American on a street corner or in a shopping mall, as Jay Leno does in his hilarious "Jay, Walking" skits, to discuss the provisions contained in the Second, Third, and Fifth, or Seventh Amendments, and you will no doubt draw blank stares or incorrect answers. Most Americans have only a rudimentary idea of their exact rights as enumerated in the Constitution. To most of us, the Constitution is a vague piece of paper, a museum piece, studied long ago in civics or history classes. In most circles the Magna Carta is unheard of.

When someone in America gets in trouble and is "read his rights," he learns quickly learns what they are. Trouble brings an appreciation for rights, and most people are smart enough to contact a lawyer and heed the attorney's advice. The American legal system is extremely complicated, and lawyers are the experts on it. When trouble arises, those in trouble expect their rights to be protected.

One right, a very important one, is the right to a speedy trial. Our forefathers did not like the idea of citizens languishing in jail for months and years before they were brought to court. The framers of our Constitution knew the importance of citizens having their day in court, the sooner the better. Yet today trials seldom occur. Rarely does the accused stand before any court to state his or her version of facts.

The jury seats in most American courtrooms are empty when felony cases find their way before a judge. Each accused person has the right to have his day in court, to present his version of the offense before a jury of his peers. The vast majority of criminal defendants, however, choose not to have their day in court. Speedy trials are more fiction than fact. A great myth in our society is that every accused criminal is vigorously defended by a tough-minded Johnnie Cochran against a determined district attorney in a packed courtroom. If every criminal defendant exercised his right to a speedy trial, the American criminal justice system would collapse in one day. There are not enough judges, courtrooms, prosecutors, or defense attorneys to handle the millions of cases that flow into the system each year. Prosecutors shy away from trials because juries are unpredictable, as evidenced by the verdict in the O.J. Simpson case. Where juries are concerned, anything can happen. Defense attorneys also shy away from trials because of the time demands and the fact that juries typically hand down harsher or more severe penalties than a defendant would typically receive in negotiated plea arrangements.

Most defendants plead guilty to the charges against them. It is very simple. Prosecutors and defense attorneys work together to process cases quickly and efficiently. In this way district attorneys obtain a high conviction rate, which looks good come election time. The more convictions, the more prosecutors can tout their effectiveness in fighting crime. Plea-bargaining also serves the interests of the accused because they typically plead guilty to a lesser offense and get out of jail sooner. Plea-bargaining benefits defense attorneys by allowing them to spend less time on each case, and the bargaining process assists judges by reducing their caseloads. Put simply, when criminal defendants "cop a plea," everyone goes along with the deal, and everyone wins. The goal of the American criminal justice system is to get cases processed and out the back door as quickly as possible. Trials, especially "speedy ones," upset the courthouse routine and expend the time and energy of everyone. Jury trials also cost a lot of money.

Death penalty cases are different—trials are the order of the day. In these cases, the State, or District Attorney presents his version of the crime. Then the defendant's attorney presents his version of the case. Like two heavyweights in a boxing ring, the attorneys go after each other. One is fighting for life, and the other is fighting for death. The judge acts like a referee and makes certain that the rules are followed. A jury watches the combatants, weighs the evidence, and reaches a conclusion. Such was the case for Hilton Crawford, who was charged with capital murder—that is, murder committed in the course of committing another felony. In Texas, a state where death penalty cases were, and still are, taken very seriously, what Crawford did was no ordinary "Friday night killing." He had allegedly murdered a defenseless child, a fact that would be emotionally very difficult to overcome. Texans have historically taken a dim view toward child murderers. Hilton was in bad company.

Between 1924 and 1972, 510 men and women in Texas were convicted of capital crimes, and 361 were eventually executed by electrical current at the Huntsville or "Walls" unit, three blocks east of the quiet Huntsville town square. The old inmate-made electric chair, called *Old Sparky*, is now in a display case in a local museum. Capital crimes during the decades in which Old Sparky served the state of Texas consisted of murder with malice aforethought, armed robbery, and rape. Juries could sentence defendants convicted of these crimes to prison terms of anywhere between five and ninety-nine years, or to death by electrocution. In June of 1972, however, the United States Supreme Court ruled in Furman v. Georgia that unbounded jury discretion led to arbitrariness because some defendants received death sentences while others convicted of the same crime under similar circumstances received prison terms. The system was not fair. The justices concluded that the death sentencing process was similar to being struck by lightning and ruled that the system of capital punishment was unconstitutional.

When the death penalty was ruled unconstitutional in the summer of 1972, there were over 600 men and women on death rows across the United States. The vast majority of these prisoners had their sentences commuted to life imprisonment. In Texas, the Furman decision resulted in the commutation of 47 death sentences.

One of these Texas Furman commutees was Kenneth McDuff, who went to prison in 1964 for burglary and was paroled in 1965. He committed three brutal murders in 1966 and received a death sentence in 1968. With the Furman decision, his sentence was commuted to life in 1972, and McDuff entered the general prison population. As a result of prison overcrowding pressures, McDuff, the prison-wise con and proverbial model prisoner, was released on parole on October 11, 1989. Within days of his release, McDuff killed again, again, and again. He was finally arrested and sentenced to death in February 1993. The monster was executed in Texas on November 17, 1998.

The Supreme Court never said the death penalty was unconstitutional, only the process and procedure by which death sentences were rendered. By September 1972, death rows across the United States had been cleared of capital offenders, who, in most instances, had their death sentences commuted to life imprisonment. The vast majority of death-row prisoners wound up in the general prison population. Some even made parole and were released to free society.

The Supreme Court left the capital-punishment door open, and in 1973 the Texas Legislature enacted a new capital-murder statute that became effective on January 1, 1974. It took less than two years to put into operation a new system of capital punishment. Lawmakers were serious about the death penalty. A number of other states followed suit. Sensitive to the language in Furman, the new Texas statute restricted a capital crime to murder in the course of another felony, such as rape, robbery, kidnapping, or burglary. The murder of a law enforcement officer was also included, and the statute was later expanded to include serial murder and mass murder. To keep up with the ever-changing kinds of murder, the Texas Legislature has modified the capital murder statute virtually every legislative session since 1974.

The case Hilton Crawford vs. The State of Texas was a high-profile one that garnered extensive local media attention. Headlines declared "Senseless killing took piece of innocence" and "Monstrous deeds: Boy's abduction-slaying joins ranks of unfathomable crimes." Reports on Hilton and his foul deeds were everywhere following his arrest on September 15. Newspaper articles even examined the effect of the crime on Conroe itself and McKay's schoolmates. From media accounts alone, it looked as if a trial and sentencing would occur in short order. The specter of a quick ending began when Hilton was formally indicted for capital murder by a Montgomery County grand jury on September 20, 1995. But this event instead signaled the start of a protracted battle among Crawford, Defense Counsel, and the Montgomery County District Attorney's Office. Even in capital cases the idea of a speedy trial is a myth.

The right to a speedy trial is guaranteed by the Sixth Amendment of the Constitution. The definition of *speedy*, however, is open to interpretation, and death penalty trials are anything but speedy. Witnesses have to be located and interviewed; physical evidence located, examined, and logged; and experts sought and retained. It takes months to gear up for a capital trial. And with this time comes expense. It has been estimated that capital-trial costs, from beginning to end, typically exceed $1 million.

Hilton Crawford's attorney wanted anything but a speedy trial. Getting Hilton in the courtroom to face the jury and account for his actions would not be easy. His defense attorneys filed a series of pre-trial motions that postponed the trial until the summer of 1996, almost a year after the crime. The prosecution, like a veteran boxer, bided their time and answered the motions one by one. One had to be patient.

While Crawford sat in the county jail, his attorneys motioned the Court to set bail. Initially, he had retained his own counsel. However, it was revealed that Crawford had filed for bankruptcy in a Houston court in May of 1995 by declaring over $300,000 in debts. The high roller and chicken importer was broke. In a November hearing Crawford's attorneys, Cynthia McMurrey of Houston and Rick Stover of Conroe, requested that District Court Judge John Martin set bail between $15,000 and $20,000. Montgomery County Prosecutor Mike Aduddell requested that bail be set at $2.5 million. Judge Martin set bail at $1 million. Carl and Paulette Everett attended the bail hearing and watched intently as Crawford, who was heavily shackled, was led into the courtroom. It was a tense meeting as Hilton briefly made eye contact with the Everetts. Paulette resisted the opportunity to speak to him. Any accidental conversations or ill words could have threatened the case. Good victims are quiet and maintain their composure; good victims are bystanders, no matter how badly their loved one has been battered or brutalized.

McMurrey protested the judge's decision, calling the $1 million bond excessive, and argued that Hilton was not a flight or escape risk. She argued that Hilton had been cooperative with the authorities, that he had provided the map to find McKay's remains. She also argued that Crawford was broke and lacked the resources to flee. Despite these pleadings, Crawford remained in jail, where he reportedly cried a lot and appeared to be depressed about his situation. During this time, law enforcement investigators ruled out third-party involvement, as the so-called R. L. Remington was never found. Hilton was now the one and only offender.

The amount of bail, however, was not the focal point of Hilton's early defense. His attorneys' major objective was securing a change of venue. Because of the extensive media coverage, the attorneys desperately wanted the trial moved to another county for Crawford to have any kind of a chance. On the heels of the bail hearing, Judge Martin issued a gag order restricting attorneys from both sides and all other participants from discussing the case. The goal of this order was to temper or restrict the amount of pre-trial publicity surrounding the case. All pre-trial hearings were moved behind closed doors to preserve Crawford's ability to receive a fair trial. The gag order was also a forward-looking strategy to reduce or eliminate an issue that could later be upheld on appeal. It was better to be cautious early than to be sorry later in the event—no matter how far-fetched—of a costly retrial. In a high-profile case anything could happen, and caution was the best strategy.

Prosecutors protested the gag order, and in December of 1995 Judge Martin modified the order to restrict only the attorneys and witnesses in the case from discussing it. The prosecutors stated that restricting the media from covering the case violated the First Amendment. Crawford's attorneys were furious at the new ruling, saying that continual media attention reduced Crawford's opportunity to receive a fair trial. The judge scheduled the trial for March 18, 1996.

The beginning of 1996 brought the usual cheer and good tidings for everyone but those enmeshed in the trial proceedings. In January of 1996, Judge Martin stepped down, citing a heavy caseload. Capital trials are time-consuming affairs, and the Crawford case, with its twists and turns and flood of meetings and motions, demanded nearly full-time attention. District Court Judge Fred Edwards stepped into the void and took over. Judge Edwards decided to relocate the trial because of the defense team's argument that the amount of pre-trial publicity was so pervasive and potentially prejudicial that

Crawford could not receive a fair trial. In February of 1996, the trial was relocated to the Criminal Justice Center on the campus of Sam Houston State University in Huntsville, Texas.

The Criminal Justice Center, dedicated in 1977, is a $7.5 million educational structure built by state prison inmates. The Center houses numerous classrooms to educate criminal justice majors, a hotel, a restaurant, and a fully functional courtroom to serve as a laboratory for criminal justice majors to observe real trials. Shortly after the building opened, the courtroom hosted a murder trial on a change of venue from Victoria, Texas, because of prejudicial testimony. The trial garnered standing-room-only crowds. The courtroom was the scene of another murder trial, this time involving two former Houston police officers charged with the death of a young prisoner in their custody. Attorneys for the ex-police officers requested a change of venue because of a great deal of pre-trial publicity. In the early 1980s the courtroom was again the scene of a murder trial on change of venue. By 1996 the campus courtroom had solid experience in hosting trials on a change of venue. Hilton Crawford's trial would be no exception, and the University agreed to host the celebrated murder trial.

Even though the trial was moved to Walker County, the population of this county, or the prospective jury pool, was also exposed to the Houston media, which continuously covered the crime and pre-trial motions of Crawford's attorneys. Walker County is home of the state prison system, and many people affiliated with the prison would be part of the jury pool. Walker County was also a conservative area, and, worse yet, the county was the site of the execution chamber. Hilton had received a change of venue, but having the trial in Walker County was probably worse than having it in his hometown. In reality it did not make any difference where the trial was held—the facts surrounding the crime were so horrifying that a jury in El Paso or Amarillo would have been outraged.

Throughout the first several months of 1996, Crawford's attorneys worked hard to obtain a bail reduction. They were successful, and the judge reset bail at $450,000. Despite this reduction, Crawford's financial position had not improved, however, so he remained in jail.

In April, the trial was set to convene in June. Crawford's attorneys filed a motion to suppress videotaped statements made by Hilton after he was charged with the kidnapping and murder.

Judge Edwards ruled otherwise and noted that Crawford's statements were in no way coerced and that he voluntarily gave what basically amounted to a confession, fully understanding his rights when he did so. Hilton's helpfulness probably helped seal his fate.

Jury selection was slated to begin in June, and the trial was reset for July. Crawford's pre-trial bag of tricks was now nearly empty. To avoid further delays, the Judge set one last pre-trial hearing, at which attorneys from either side were to raise any remaining issues for final consideration. Crawford's counsel raised the insanity defense, but Judge Edwards denied the motion. Paulette had a good laugh when she heard this. She said, "Hilton was nuts all right, but not in the legal sense."

During the pretrial motion phase, Carl and Paulette drove back and forth to Mississippi to visit relatives and friends. It was good to get away and think about something else. They had no control over the pre-trial show and were in reality bit players in a larger movie. It was out of their hands, and all they could do was watch.

In late June, roughly 500 prospective jurors from the Huntsville area were issued summonses to report for jury duty. After the jury pool completed a questionnaire, the group was reduced to 100 qualified jurors. This pool completed an additional twenty-page questionnaire as part of the selection process. Both sides reviewed the information, and on July 1, 1996, a jury of eight women and four men was finally seated. Two female alternates were also selected. The "Trial of the Century" was about to begin.

Jury selection was not without some drama. One day, both Crawford and Paulette entered the courtroom at almost the same time. Hilton sat near his counsels' table, but his chair was near the half-fence separating the audience from the court personnel. Paulette sat down in the front row of the audience seating area, mere inches away from the fence. They were close together, so close that Hilton leaned toward Paulette and, with their faces just inches apart, whispered, "Fuck you."

Paulette smiled and said, "And good morning to you too." The two adversaries were quickly separated like boxers in the ring. Paulette was startled by the hate and anger in Hilton's face and eyes. In Paulette's mind, Hilton was like a trapped animal filled with rage. She wondered what McKay saw in his face in those last moments.

The prosecution revealed that they had a list of 200 potential witnesses to call for the trial, which was scheduled to begin on July 8. It looked like the "Trial of the Century" would take a century. Paulette was braced for a long and emotional ordeal. Every day she would have to relive the crime and revisit her agonizing grief.

Chapter 5

Trial of the Century

It seemed like it took forever to get the trial started. The crime committed by Hilton against my child was fresh in my mind. I wanted the trial to happen right away so no one would forget about what happened to my child. Well, that did not happen, but when that trial date was set I was glad. I was so glad because now the whole world was going to see what that demon did to my baby. I just wanted justice for McKay. I knew those jurors would give Hilton the justice he deserved. I also knew that I had to be strong. I had to control my anger because I was going to testify in court. I was to relive the whole nightmare again. I had to sit and listen to how and why that demon murdered my child. The more I thought about it, the more I knew I had to do it. I had to sit there and be quiet for McKay's sake. I would get my chance to talk on the witness stand. I was going to tell my story and do it face to face with Hilton. I was going to tell him how much we all hurt now because of him. I was ready, and I wanted him to hear what I had to say.

After nine months of skirmishes, the two opposing sides were about to argue the case Hilton Crawford vs. The State of Texas. One side was arguing to save the life of Hilton, and the other side was arguing for the execution of Hilton. The headlines of the Conroe Courier on Sunday, July 7, 1996, read, "Trial of the Century Finally at Hand." The trial of Nathan Leopold and Richard Loeb, also termed the "Crime of the Century," had begun on Monday, July 21, 1924, almost exactly 72 years before Crawford's trial. In both cases, one side argued for revenge and justice, while the other side pleaded for mercy and life.

The courtroom in the Criminal Justice Center, roughly 5,000

square feet, is an imposing room. It is fitted with 112 spectator seats, 56 on either side of an aisle that leads down to a swinging half-door providing entrance and exit to the tables for opposing counsel, the jury box, the judge's bench and desk area, witness stand, and the court reporter's box. The courtroom also has state-of-the-art technology to show evidence videos. Near the courtroom are rooms to sequester the jury, witness waiting rooms, and judges' chambers. The setting for the drama was ready. The press anticipated a grand story.

On Monday, July 8, Defense Counsel and the prosecution waived the opportunity to make opening statements before the jury was sworn in. After the jury was seated and sworn in, the judge instructed members not to discuss the case among themselves until they had heard all of the evidence. Among other things, they were instructed to listen and to consider all of the evidence carefully before arriving at a verdict. They were asked to be fair and impartial. Once these instructions were discussed, the State read the indictment against Hilton Crawford:

> On or about September 12, 1995, in Montgomery County, Texas, Hilton Lewis Crawford, hereinafter called the defendant, did then and there intentionally cause the death of an individual, named Samuel McKay Everett, by shooting him with a deadly weapon, to wit, a firearm, and by striking said Samuel McKay Everett with an object unknown to the Grand Jury or by a combination of both such acts, and the defendant was then and there in the course of committing and attempting to commit the offense of kidnapping of Samuel McKay Everett, against the peace and dignity of the State.

There it was, in the most straightforward language, the case against Hilton Crawford. The judge then asked: "What says the defendant?"

Standing with his back to the audience, Hilton proclaimed, "Not guilty."

After Hilton's plea, the prosecutor made an opening statement:

Ladies and gentlemen of the jury, lock the door and turn

on the alarm. That is the last thing Paulette Everett told her son, McKay. Don't talk to strangers. Don't open the door for a stranger. Don't let a stranger in the house. You don't know what evil lurks in the heart of a stranger. The evidence will show, however, that evil toward McKay lurked not in the heart of a stranger, but behind the face of a friend, the face of Hilton Crawford. Uncle Hilty, as McKay called him, was a long-time family friend.

This case is about a child's trust and the betrayal of that trust. This case is about the ultimate betrayal. But the evidence will show that Samuel McKay Everett is dead because of somebody he trusted. Somebody he knew. He trusted Hilton Crawford.

The prosecutor told the jury the facts of the case, including what specific witnesses would testify to, and closed with the following statement:

McKay Everett is dead. I expect that the evidence will prove beyond a reasonable doubt that McKay was kidnapped from his home in Montgomery County, Texas, by Hilton Crawford, in Hilton Crawford's gold-colored Chrysler with the Crown Motors sticker on the back; that McKay Everett was struck by Hilton Crawford in the head while he was in the trunk of the defendant's car; that McKay Everett was shot by the defendant, Hilton Crawford; that twelve-year-old McKay Everett is dead because Hilton Crawford wanted a half a million dollars. McKay Everett is dead.

The prosecutor's opening statement—direct, fact-filled, and powerful—provided the jury with a synopsis of the case. It was also filled with details that foreshadowed the prosecution's strategy. The jury heard about betrayal, the Amway meeting, the home security system, Uncle Hilty, Highway I-10, Whiskey Bay, and McKay's damaged body. These fragments of information resembled pieces of a large, complex puzzle that the prosecution would be assembling for the jury. The opening statement left Hilton no time, not one second, to take a breath.

The prosecutor started the trial aggressively and showed the Court that there would be no respite from an impending avalanche of evidence.

The prosecutor's first witness was Paulette. When her name was called aloud, the audience hushed in anticipation of the coming testimony. Tension filled the room as Paulette stood up and began to slowly make her way toward the witness stand. She felt her body stiffen, and the bailiff had to help her reach the witness chair. It took a few moments, and every muscle in her body, for her to take the stand, but in those seconds Paulette relived the entire tragedy again. The movie in her mind replayed the events of September 12, 1995. A split second later she wanted to break away from the bailiff and run at Hilton and claw him to pieces, and scream, scream, and scream. But she reminded herself to be a good victim, to remain calm and resolute.

In preparation for her testimony, Paulette had been advised to dress plainly, avoid the use of excessive make-up, and refrain from wearing flashy jewelry or shoes. She wore an old dress. The strategy was intended for the jurors to focus on Paulette and her story, not her apparel. The District Attorney stood up. The horror story was set to unfold.

Before the first question was asked, Paulette looked past the prosecutor and gazed at Hilton. The two adversaries came face-to-face. To Paulette, he seemed dazed and remote. His moved in slow motion. She wanted to see him in prison garb, but he wore a suit instead. She asked herself, "Why do we scrub up a crocodile, a child killer, to look like one of us, when he murdered a child?"

Paulette was jerked back to reality as the prosecutor asked a series of simple and direct questions about her and Carl.

The District Attorney showed Paulette a picture while asking her to identify the person in the picture, to which she replied, "That's my baby." She then responded to questions about her relationship with Connie and Hilton Crawford. She told the jury that the Crawfords came to see McKay shortly after he was born and that Hilton even held the infant boy. Paulette said, "McKay was so close to the Crawfords that he referred to them as 'Aunt Connie and Uncle Hilty'."

The most important questions surfaced when Paulette told the

Court about the events preceding the Amway meeting on September 12, 1995. She testified that she received a phone call around 5 p.m. from Hilton Crawford, who was checking to see if she and Carl still planned to attend the Amway meeting. She said he also wanted to know if the meeting location was still at the bank building in downtown Conroe. She testified that she answered "yes" to all of Hilton's questions. Paulette also stated that Hilton had called and asked her the same basic questions the week before. He replied that he would see them at the meeting.

Paulette answered the questions in a very slow, methodical way. She wanted to communicate the information to the jury in the clearest and most concise fashion possible. This was no time to emote, to get upset, or to forget some important fact or detail. It was time to give McKay a voice. The questions returned to McKay, and Paulette told the Court that on September 12 McKay wore denim shorts, a T-shirt, and tennis shoes. She told the Court that Randy Bartlett, a neighbor, called her and asked for a ride to the Amway meeting. She also stated that she and Bartlett left McKay sitting in his favorite chair, smiling through a mouthful of braces, eating vanilla ice cream from the carton. They drove away around 8:00 p.m.

Then there were more questions about the Amway meeting. Paulette stated that the meeting ended around 10 p.m. and that Hilton was a no-show. She talked about going to a nearby restaurant with a group of people from the meeting. It was at the restaurant, she said, that Carl tried to call McKay. She said that Carl, concerned that McKay did not answer the phone, left the restaurant and went home to check on him. Paulette told the Court that as Randy Bartlett drove her home, he informed her that her son was missing and that she screamed all the way home.

Paulette was pleased to tell the jury her version of the events, but to do so, she had to relive the entire episode again. The prosecution was finished, but now she had to endure cross-examination by Crawford's attorneys. The defense asked Paulette to sketch on a blackboard their back driveway. Her picture showed that the lane was long and winding and that it snaked through a heavily wooded lot.

Paulette was asked about McKay's friends, what they liked to do, and where they liked to play in the neighborhood. She testified about the alarm system in the house, how proficient McKay was with it, and how close the Everett and Crawford families were. So close that Hilton frequently gave McKay gifts like basketballs, footballs, and gum. The cross-examination was nearing completion when the defense attorney asked Paulette, "Was there anything else that was notable about McKay's relationship with Mr. Crawford prior to September 12 of 1995?" Paulette calmly replied, "My son loved him." She answered a few more questions and then stepped down.

Testifying against Hilton was a major milestone in Paulette's recovery. She left the witness stand exhausted and, as Mississippians say, "limp as rainwater." She wanted to run away, just get away from the spotlight. It had taken everything she had to recount the events of that day and the events leading up to McKay's murder. It had taken courage she did not know she had to sit alone on the witness stand and come face to face with her child's killer, and this confrontation would not be the last time. Over the years, through the trial and beyond, her life and Hilton's would continue to zig and zag like a pair of country roads. Sometimes the two roads would be miles apart, and then suddenly, they would unexpectedly intersect and then drift apart again. The trial was an intersection of their roads. It would take several more years before the roads would finally drift apart altogether.

Next on the witness stand was Randy Bartlett, the neighbor of the Everetts who had attended the Amway meeting with Paulette that night. He testified that he had known Hilton for five or six years and brought the Everetts into the Amway business.

Turning to the events of September 12, Bartlett was asked, "Around 7:40 p.m., did anything happen at your home?" The neighbor told the Court, "I received a phone call at my home that was a hang-up call or, you know, not a received call, at approximately 7:40 p.m." He said that after the call he walked over to the Everett house to get a ride with Paulette to the meeting. His responses planted a very important seed in the jury's mind. Someone, perhaps Hilton, had called Bartlett before the Amway meeting to see if anyone was home.

Bartlett told the Court that he and Paulette left the Everett residence around 8 p.m. He also stated that Crawford was a no-show at the meeting. After the Amway get-together, a few friends gathered at a restaurant for coffee. Bartlett told the Court that while there, he observed Carl Everett make a phone call from a pay phone. After the call, at or about 11:00 p.m., Carl excused himself and went home. Bartlett continued, saying that Bill Kahn, another neighbor, had called him at the restaurant and told him that McKay was missing and that he needed to bring Paulette home. In the car he told Paulette about Kahn's phone call, and she became hysterical. After she had regained her composure, Bartlett said he drove Paulette home. At the same time that they arrived, a Montgomery County Sheriff's Department patrol car, with two officers, drove up.

Bartlett was asked what he remembered Carl Everett saying to him.

"Someone's got my son. I need to call someone for help. Who can I call to help us?" said Bartlett.

Bartlett testified that Carl was in a state of hysteria and he had to take him back into the house to try to calm him down and get him to explain what was going on. While Bartlett was in the house with Carl, other law enforcement officers began to arrive, including Tony Wargo of the FBI. The questioning turned back to McKay and an event that had occurred several years prior to the abduction. Bartlett told the Court that one time when McKay was alone in his house, an alarm went off and alerted the sheriff's department. A deputy was dispatched to investigate, and he knocked on the back door of the Everetts' residence. Bartlett said that when the young man in the house refused to open the door, the deputy came over to his house and explained the situation. The neighbor told the deputy, "The young man has been instructed not to open the doors for strangers. His behavior is not unusual."

Later the prosecutor asked if Bartlett had given Wargo a list of names of people he knew who owned gold Chryslers, and he replied "Yes." The prosecutor followed up and asked Bartlett if he had also provided Wargo with a list of people who were at the Amway meeting that night and also people who had been invited but did not show. Bartlett again replied in the affirmative. After this response, the prosecution asked him, "Did you also take part in providing Mr. Wargo with a list of people that you felt McKay would open the door for or deactivate the security system for?"

Bartlett echoed himself, "Yes."

The prosecution narrowed in, asking, "And was the defendant's name on any of these lists?"

Bartlett answered, "Yes."

Sensing the kill, the prosecutor pushed on. "To your knowledge, during that time, were there any other people's names, any other individual's name that made all three lists of these people?"

"Not to my knowledge," Bartlett said.

Randy Bartlett's testimony was devastating in serving up Hilton as the perpetrator. In tennis parlance, it looked like "game, set, and match." However, the prosecution was ready with reams of additional testimony and physical evidence. Even though it was early in the trial, it did not look good for Hilton.

The next witness was a school friend of McKay's, Elizabeth Schaeffer, who was thirteen at the time of the kidnapping and murder. Elizabeth and McKay had been seventh graders at Peet Junior High in Conroe.

"How long had you known McKay before September of last year?" the District Attorney asked.

Elizabeth replied, "Three years."

She was then asked, "Would you consider yourself a good friend of McKay's?"

"Yes," she said.

Probing the depth of their friendship, the prosecutor, inquired, "How often do you think you would talk to McKay?"

Elizabeth said, "Every day."

"On September 12, 1995, did you talk to McKay on the phone?"

"Yes, he called me."

"Do you know what time he called you?"

"About 8:30 p.m.," Elizabeth stated to the Court. She testified that during the communication with McKay she briefly put the phone down to exchange some magazines and catalogues with a friend who had stopped by. After a few seconds, she returned to her conversation with McKay.

Shortly after their conversation resumed, McKay asked Elizabeth to hold on, to wait a moment. Elizabeth testified that she heard McKay set down the phone and open the door. It was the back door by the garage, the one at the end of the heavily wooded driveway. She heard him open the door. Elizabeth said that she looked at the clock on her phone and it said 8:31 p.m.

"What happened next?"

"I had a beep on the other line. I have call waiting, so I clicked over and I talked, then I clicked back over and he still wasn't there, so I just hung up."

"Did you try calling McKay again?"

"Yes, about fifteen or thirty minutes later."

"Did you get a response?"

Elizabeth said yes, but the line was busy and she gave up calling him back. The Schaeffer household retired for the evening after the news, around 10:30 p.m.

Perhaps the most unnerving part of Elizabeth's testimony involved her answer to this seemingly harmless question: "Where do you live, Elizabeth?"

"I live at 312 South Rivershire." Right next door to Hilton and Connie Crawford. Elizabeth had grown up around the Crawfords and had seen McKay at the Crawford house.

Bill Kahn, the neighbor who lived across the street from the Everetts, testified next that as he was putting out his trash cans, around 8:30 p.m. on September 12, he saw a car enter the Everetts' driveway and drive up to the house. It was summertime and just light enough for Kahn to identify the car as a Chrysler, though he did not notice the color. Kahn then returned to his house, where his wife handed him additional garbage, which he took back out to the trash cans. Kahn testified that while he was standing by the trash cans he saw the same car backing out from the Everetts' driveway. The car backed out into the street and stopped just short of hitting his trash cans.

"What did you notice about the car?"

Kahn told the Court, "I noticed it was a Chrysler product, and a gold or bronze in color and had a Crown Motors emblem and a Crown sticker on the trunk, on the left side." Kahn indicated that he knew these things because the back-up lights gave off just enough illumination for him to see the make and color of the vehicle. He also testified that the vehicle's tinted windows prohibited him from seeing anything within the car.

"Did you hear any yelling, screaming, or anything?"

Kahn replied, "No, sir," and said that the vehicle's arrival and departure from the Everett home took place in three or four minutes.

He noted that the Chrysler drove away down the street at "a pretty rapid rate of speed." Later that evening, Kahn said, he told law enforcement officials about what he had seen.

Kahn also testified that law enforcement officers took him on September 14, 1995, to a local auto dealer to see if he could identify a car that resembled the one that he had seen on the 12th. He was able to, and the specific vehicle was a Chrysler LHS. A short time later, Kahn was taken to the FBI offices in The Woodlands, a town just south of Conroe, and shown a car. According to Kahn, the car was the one he had seen enter and leave the Everett residence. This auto, however, was missing the Crown Motors emblem and the Crown sticker. Even though the sticker was gone, he could tell where the sticker had been removed.

"As far as you were concerned, that was the same vehicle that you had seen on the Tuesday night previous?"

Kahn said, "Yes, sir."

"Do you have any doubt in your mind?"

Again, Kahn spoke with confidence: "None whatsoever."

Defense Counsel tried to chip away at Kahn's testimony by suggesting that it had been too dark to see anything or that he had been too far away from the vehicle to make a positive identification. But Kahn was resolute. His testimony placed a gold LHS Chrysler at the Everett residence around 8:30 p.m. on September 12.

Carl Everett was next. The prosecution wasted little time in getting Carl to discuss his relationship with the Crawfords. He said that he and Paulette had considered the Crawfords friends and that they saw each other several times a year. The two families often tried to get together around the holidays. Most of the get-togethers were at the Crawford residence.

"Had you and McKay been over to the Crawford residence, say in the last two months preceding September 12, 1995?"

Carl replied, "Yes sir. Three weeks prior to the events of September 12, Hilton came out on the driveway and passed the football around with McKay quite a bit and then got the basketball out and they shot some hoops." Carl stated that they stayed at the Crawford residence for two hours or so.

The District Attorney proceeded to ask Carl about the events of September 12. Carl said that he and Paulette left McKay at home so that he could finish his homework while they attended the Amway meeting. Carl's testimony about the meeting and get-together at the restaurant confirmed the stories of the previous witnesses.

"On the way to the restaurant, did you make any phone calls?"

"Yes sir, I have a mobile phone and I called my home to check on McKay." Carl testified that he received no response and that he thought this was unusual, but not out of the ordinary. Carl called home from a pay phone at the restaurant and still could not reach McKay. He felt that something was not right at that point, so he told Paulette and the others that he was going home.

The drive from the restaurant to the Everett residence took maybe eight to ten minutes. During this short drive, Carl testified that he called home a third time and still received no response from McKay. Carl drove up the wooded driveway, and as he neared the house he saw the back door standing open six to eight inches. He thought that this was unusual. Carl parked his truck, entered the house, and called out for McKay.

"What did you do after you walked in and hollered for McKay?"

Carl offered, "I walked down that hallway that you're at when you walk through that door, and about the time I got to the family room, the phone started ringing. I never broke stride. I walked straight into the kitchen and answered the phone. There was a lady's voice, a kind of rusty, rough-sounding voice. I had never heard this voice before. She said, 'Who is this?' and I said, "This is Carl Everett."

"What happened then?"

Carl told the Court that she asked, 'Where is your son?'

"I said, 'Well, he better be here doing his homework, eating his dinner.' She said 'Well, he's not, we have him.' I said, 'Who is we?' She said, 'Well it's we—*we* got him.'"

"What else did she say?"

Carl replied, "She said if you want your son back alive, there's going to be money involved." I said, 'Money?' She said, 'We have your son and if you want to see him alive, it's going to cost you $500,000 and it's going to be bundled in $10,000 bundles of hundred-dollar bills,' and she said, 'If you call the police, you won't see him alive again.'"

"What did you say?"

Carl kept telling his story as if it had happened just the other day and said, "Well, I want to talk to him. I want to know he's okay. She said, 'You ain't going to fucking talk to him no more,' and she hung up."

Carl stated that after she hung up he called out for McKay. He thought it might have been a prank, but the voice sounded serious. He called the Bartletts to see if McKay was there and he was not. "I started screaming for McKay, screaming his name, and I went outside looking for him." Carl stated that when he went back into the empty house, he dialed 911.

He remembered that he placed the emergency call at approximately 11:15 p.m.

"What happened next?"

Carl said, "Bill Kahn called the restaurant where my wife was, and I went all through my house, through our bedroom, and even looked under the beds. I was hoping he was there." A short time later two deputies from the Montgomery County Sheriff's department arrived. He told them what had happened and gave them the usual information concerning names, dates, phone numbers, and addresses. It was impossible to believe. Crime and crime scenes and detectives were things that he had read about in the newspaper, seen on television, or heard about on the radio. And now the Everett residence had been transformed from a home, a child's home, into a crime scene.

Carl testified that around 11:45 p.m., after he talked to the deputies, he went inside the house to call his friend Hilton. The District Attorney wanted to know who picked up the phone. Carl said that Connie Crawford was on the other end. Carl asked if Hilton was there, but she wanted to know what was going on. He told her that someone had taken McKay and that a lady called wanting money. Carl also told Connie that he needed Hilton to come over and help him. Connie replied that Hilton was not there and that she had not seen him. Carl asked Connie to give him Hilton's mobile phone number so that he could contact him. Connie told Carl that she did not know her husband's mobile number. She told Carl that if she heard from Hilton she would tell him to call him. This conversation lasted about thirty seconds.

Carl described the events that followed. The unsecured crime scene began to fill with people. Friends and neighbors arrived at the Everett residence. It was now a serious situation. More deputies from the Sheriff's Department came; so did members of the Federal Bureau of Investigation. Throughout the night, Carl was interviewed by these police officials. It was one battery of questions after another, question and answer, question and answer, like a verbal machine gun. It was grueling and relentless. But the sequence of events had to be established and validated.

Having established events of the evening, the District Attorney shifted gears and asked, "Did McKay trust the defendant?"

Carl said, "Yes, sir, he did." Carl also told the Court that McKay was very experienced in the operation of their home's security system. In fact, Carl said that McKay knew how to operate the security system better than he or Paulette.

The questions were now following a familiar pattern—like a river flowing to the ocean, the outcome was inevitable.

"Do you feel like McKay would have opened that door for a stranger?"

Carl said that McKay would never have opened the door for a stranger.

"Do you feel like McKay would have opened the door for Hilton Lewis Crawford?"

Carl told the court, "Yes, I do." The witness also stated that his son would not have opened the door for a uniformed guard or uniformed officer. The boy had been raised never to open the door for a stranger.

"Why did you call Hilton Crawford that evening after you got the ransom call?"

"I knew Hilton's background in law enforcement and the security company that he managed," Carl told the court, "and I knew he had the background that might be able to help me. I knew he had been a deputy sheriff in Jefferson County. I knew he had training in security and law enforcement."

Although it was a difficult task, Defense Counsel probed Carl about the relationship between his family and the Crawfords. The defense attorney wanted to know why, when the Everetts and Crawfords got together, it was usually at the Crawfords' place. Carl told Hilton's attorney that he had invited the Crawfords over several times but that things never worked out. Schedule conflicts came up. Carl did say that at Hilton's request, the Everetts had hosted a surprise birthday party at their house for Connie. Overall, and to Carl's best recollection, Hilton had been to their house about five times prior to September 12.

The defense attorney asked Carl about the ransom call. Carl told the lawyer that the caller said that she knew he had a mobile phone and she wanted that number. He gave her the number because she said she was going to call him at 8:00 a.m. the next day to provide instructions as to what to do with the ransom money.

When the defense attorney was through examining Carl, the District Attorney had a final question for him. "Did you ever receive another ransom call instructing you what to do with the money?"

"No, sir," replied Carl.

Christina Caplan, the custodian of the tapes of emergency calls for Montgomery County, was the last witness in what had been a long emotional day. She testified that the first emergency call from the Everett residence on September 12, 1995, was at 11:16 p.m. and lasted just over five minutes. Her testimony on the time of the 911 call confirmed Carl's story.

Day two in the "Trial of the Century" began with the testimony of Thomas Taylor, a deputy with the Montgomery County Sheriff's Department. Taylor testified that in August of 1994, he was dispatched to the Everett residence to respond to an alarm. He stated that he approached the back door, by the three-car garage, parked his official vehicle, and rang the buzzer. He said that McKay came to the door but that the head behind the door shook sideways. Taylor, in uniform, asked the boy a second time to open the door, but again he shook his head. Taylor asked McKay if everything was okay, and he said yes. This critical point was not lost on the jury. McKay, as he'd been taught, refused to open the door even for a uniformed law enforcement officer with a marked car in plain view.

Bruce Zenor, another sheriff's deputy, testified that he was dispatched to the Everett home on September 12, 1995, in regards to a possible kidnapping. He said that he arrived at the residence around 11:40 p.m. and that he and another deputy were the first law enforcement officials on the scene.

"What happened next?"

Mr. Everett, Zenor replied, told them that he had received a phone call from an unknown woman who stated that "they had his son and requested a large amount of money if he ever wanted to see his son alive again."

"How was Mr. Everett acting at that time?"

Zenor told the court that Carl was very upset and that he nearly collapsed after telling the deputies his story. The deputy testified that Carl showed them the open door at the rear of the house. At this point, Zenor and the deputy notified their supervisors that a child was missing and it appeared that an abduction had occurred.

"Then what did you do?"

The deputy told the court that he proceeded to place cones in the driveway and cordon off the area with yellow crime-scene tape. Although there were friends' cars in the driveway and people in the house, the deputies did their best to protect the area as a crime scene. Zenor said that following this procedure, he entered the house and told the people there to stay out of the kitchen because it was part of a crime scene. He said they sealed it off as best they could. Zenor also told the court that he walked through the house and saw no signs of forced entry. Other law enforcement officials arrived around 1:50 a.m. and Zenor said they turned the crime scene over to them.

Defense counsel asked Zenor a few questions about possible contamination of the crime scene due to the friends and neighbors who came by and milled around the kitchen.

Norbert LeBlanc, a latent-print examiner for the Sheriff's Department, followed Deputy Zenor. He said he arrived at the Everett residence around 1:26 a.m. on September 13 and that one of the deputies on the scene informed him of the events on the evening before. LeBlanc told the court that he photographed the residence, dusted various areas for fingerprints, and preserved several footprints and tire-print impressions, which were possibly left by the kidnappers. He left about two hours later.

LeBlanc testified that on Thursday, September 14, he was asked by an FBI agent investigating the case to come to the FBI office and take a look at a car they thought was used in the kidnapping. LeBlanc's tire impressions, lifted from the Everett residence driveway, did not match the 1994 Chrysler LHS he was shown. LeBlanc did notice, though, that an emblem on the trunk of the gold LHS had been recently removed.

"Who else was with you when you were examining the car?"

"Hilton Crawford was there," replied LeBlanc. "He was not under arrest and he was not handcuffed."

LeBlanc said that at this point an FBI agent requested that the Montgomery County Sheriff's Department impound the car for further investigation.

"Was Mr. Crawford aware the car was being taken into custody?"

"Yes, he did give verbal consent. He said, 'Yes, you have my permission to take the car.' He just requested that he get something out of the trunk and out of the interior of the car."

"And when you opened the trunk, did you see inside the trunk?"

"Yes sir, there was no carpet or anything in the trunk. The trunk was very empty. Except for a briefcase, a black briefcase, or large bag, there was nothing inside the trunk, which I could tell."

LeBlanc and his colleagues began the search of Hilton's Chrysler around 4:00 p.m. on September 14. The print examiner told the court that the search uncovered assorted papers, sunglasses, other items, and clothing from the cleaners hanging behind the driver's side of the vehicle. They collected a Motorola pager, gasoline receipts, and two cellular phones—one was in Crawford's name, the other in his wife's.

"Did the car itself, the exterior of the car, did it look clean?"

LeBlanc testified that the LHS was very clean. He said "The car, the tires, themselves, looked like they had recently been 'Armor All protected' and the car looked like it had been recently detailed—it was cleaned very completely from inside and out." LeBlanc further stated that he dusted the car's interior and exterior for prints. He found a few palm prints belonging to Hilton on the exterior of the trunk.

LeBlanc explained to the court that on September 15 at 8:15 a.m. he and several other deputies executed an evidentiary search warrant at Crawford's Conroe residence. They collected a Motorola pager, gasoline receipts, and two cellular phones.

"Can you tell the jury the notations that are made on the gas card receipts?"

LeBlanc stated, "The date was September 12, 1995, at 8:55

p.m. The location on the receipt was Diamond Shamrock #2 in Conroe, Texas."

LeBlanc was asked to examine a second gas receipt. He said that this receipt was dated September 13, 1995, and timed at 7:50 a.m. "The location was another Diamond Shamrock, but this time the location was in Lumberton, a small Texas town a few miles north of Beaumont."

Hilton's attorneys asked LeBlanc about the fingerprints and shoe prints that he had examined at the crime scene. He said that the shoe prints did not match any of the shoes that they found at Crawford's residence. The crime scene investigator also told the court that the palm print he found on the trunk of the LHS was Hilton's, but that a palm print on one's own car trunk was not unusual—Crawford had legitimate access to his own vehicle and trunk.

After Norbert LeBlanc came Tony Wargo of the FBI. Wargo said that in the early morning hours of September 13, 1995, he received a call from his office about a possible kidnapping in Conroe. He went immediately to the Everett residence and found that there were other FBI agents and uniformed deputies from the Sheriff's department already on the scene.

"Was the scene under control?"

Wargo informed the court that the scene was not under control, as there were people everywhere inside and outside of the residence. "People," he said "had access to everything. The first thing I tried to do was help get the scene under control. We went into the house and tried to get as many people out of the house that really did not need to be there and get them over to a neighbor's house. For a short period it worked, but people again started coming back into the house."

"What was your duty at the Everett residence?"

Wargo replied that he talked to Carl Everett and tried to get as many details from him as he could.

"At some time during the investigation were Carl and Paulette excluded as possible suspects?"

In kidnapping investigations, the parents are always regarded as possible suspects. The process of elimination that unfolds basically proceeds from the inside out. Wargo told the court that the Everetts were excluded as suspects within the first twenty-four hours of the investigation.

The prosecution asked Wargo if any lists of possible suspects were made based on interviews and discussion with people at the scene.

Wargo confirmed that he had made a list of people who were no-shows at the Amway meeting the previous evening. He made another list of people who had access to a vehicle like the one seen entering and leaving the Everett residence on the 12th. Wargo's final list contained the names of people that McKay trusted and for whom he would have opened the door if requested.

The prosecutor wanted to know if anyone's name surfaced on all three lists. Wargo said one name emerged on all of the lists: Hilton Crawford.

"To the best of your knowledge, did anybody else's name make all three lists other than Hilton Crawford's?"

The FBI agent replied, "Not to my knowledge."

The defense asked Wargo about the crime scene as he found it on his arrival. Wargo reiterated that the house was in a state of chaos. He told the court that he and his personnel did not want Carl and Paulette talking to their neighbors and friends because the crime was still fresh and they were looking for suspects. He said that everyone was a suspect and he could not rule out anything or anybody.

Chris Siffert with the Houston Cellular Telephone Company followed Wargo. Siffert, a fraud-control manager for the company, was responsible for detecting unauthorized usage of mobile phones by individual customers. He testified that he had been asked to produce phone records for the FBI concerning a specific number. The mobile number was Hilton's, and the records showed that on September 12, between 12:01 a.m. and 11:59 p.m., nine outgoing calls were placed. The phone records also displayed the number called; the time the call was placed; the hour, minute, and second; the locations; the actual duration of each call; and the origin of the call. Cell phones are nice conveniences, but they can also pinpoint a person's location when calls are made.

Mike Wheat of Houston Cellular offered additional information about the phone calls made from Hilton's cell phone on September 12. Wheat pegged each call to a specific location in

Texas. Marnie Cruz, also of Houston Cellular, testified that four calls made from Hilton's cell phone were made from the Lake Charles, Louisiana, area. The dots concerning Hilton's whereabouts were being connected.

And so, day two of the highly publicized "Trial of the Century" ended. For those who were keeping score, the day went to the prosecution. Effectively, the State showed that McKay had a strong relationship with Hilton Crawford; that McKay even affectionately called him "Uncle Hilty"; that Hilton had been to the Everetts' home on several occasions; that McKay turned off the security system, opened the back door, and left with someone he knew; that a gold Chrysler LHS entered and exited the Everett residence around 8:30 p.m.; that Hilton's car had recently been "detailed" and that the trunk lining was missing; and that Hilton's mobile phone records showed a number of calls placed from locations between Conroe and Lake Charles, Louisiana, on the evening of September 12, 1995. Defense counsel tried to poke holes in these facts, but the chain of evidence and case testimony was gaining momentum toward a predictable outcome.

Day three of the guilt-innocence phase began with the testimony of Bambi Carter, night auditor of the Best Western in Beaumont where Crawford had checked in. She told the court that she worked the 11 p.m. to 7 a.m. shift on September 13, 1995.

"Do you remember a man by the name of Hilton Crawford?"

Ms. Carter said she did. She had remembered the name because she thought it was unusual. She testified that Crawford checked into the hotel sometime after 4 a.m. A credit card receipt signed by Hilton validated her testimony. She also noted that Crawford had filled out the hotel registration form, including the make of his car and the tags.

As in a television thriller, the prosecutor then asked Ms. Carter, "Do you recognize the man in the courtroom today that checked in September 13, 1995?"

Ms. Carter replied, "Yes, he's the man wearing a suit, and he's sitting at the table in front of me."

Ms. Wathen, another Best Western employee, verified that

Crawford checked out at 7:33 a.m. on September 13. She also testified that Hilton was billed for two in-room telephone calls, one to his wife, Connie, at 6:35 a.m. and one at 7:24 a.m. to Bill Kahn.

Defense counsel attempted to cast doubt on the accuracy of the receipts and time of Hilton's movements.

Billy Allen, a long-time friend of Hilton's, testified that Crawford had tried to call him on the morning of September 13, 1995, while he was en route from his residence in Buna, Texas, to Lumberton and Jasper to mow grass around some storage sheds. Allen testified that he called the Crawford residence around 7:30 a.m. and that Connie answered the phone. She gave Billy a number where Hilton could be reached, but Allen testified that he did not know whether the number was for a mobile phone or a pager.

The discrepancy was not lost on the jury or the courtroom audience. Carl Everett had testified the day before that when he called the Crawford residence the night of the kidnapping in search of Hilton, Connie had told him that she did not know where Hilton was and did not have a phone number for contacting him.

Allen continued, telling the court that around 9 a.m. a friend of his, Gary Capo, drove up and they started talking. Then, a few minutes later, Hilton arrived on the scene in his car, a gold Chrysler. Allen said Capo left and Hilton asked him if he could put some belongings in a storage room.

"Then what happened?"

Allen replied, "Hilton seemed concerned about the fact that he placed a guard on duty at a job in Houston. The guard was not certified to carry a weapon, but he allowed the guard to carry his gun. The guard caught somebody breaking into the building and the guy shot at the guard and the guard was nicked in the arm and the other fellow got away. Hilton said he [the guard] was not hurt seriously but if anybody found out about the gun, he might lose his security license and his business." Hilton told Allen that he had made the guard get into his trunk so as not to get his car bloody and he drove him to the guard's parents' house.

"Then what happened?"

Allen testified that Hilton drove his car between a couple of storage sheds and started taking things out of the vehicle. Allen also said that he gave Hilton a screwdriver so that he could take the liner out of the trunk.

"Did you see the lining of the trunk?"

Allen told the court that he had observed three or four little spots of what he thought was blood. The bloodstains were the size of silver dollars.

"What was Crawford doing?"

Allen stated that "Hilton was using some cleaner on the spots, he was trying to get the spots out."

"Then what happened?"

Allen said that Hilton took out the bottom portion of the trunk lining.

Billy Allen further testified that he saw Hilton remove a bag, several other items, and a gun from the trunk. He said that Hilton gave him the gun.

"Can you describe for the jury the gun that he gave you?"

Billy Allen was a very helpful witness. He said the gun was a .45. He said that he placed the gun in a sack and that Crawford then placed the sack in the storage building.

"Then what happened?"

Allen told the court that Hilton said he had to get back home and handed him a bottle of champagne wrapped in a towel. Allen said that he thought the trunk lining, or what looked like a carpet, was of no use to Hilton, so he tossed it into a fire to get rid of it. He did not know that it was evidence of any crime. Crawford left after about thirty minutes.

The defense, among other things, asked Allen about the time sequence and the bottle of champagne. He told the court that he thought nothing about the champagne because Hilton had given him and his wife bottles of champagne in the past.

Roger Humphrey, an FBI agent, testified next that on September 15, 1995, he picked up Billy Allen at his residence in Buna and drove to the storage sheds in Lumberton. Allen unlocked shed #124 and they looked into a green garbage bag that Crawford had left at the facility.

"What did you find in the garbage bag?"

Humphrey said he found a gun in the bag, a Smith and Wesson .45 caliber pistol that was fully loaded. The gun, Humphrey said, "also had what appeared to be bloodstains on it." The stains were on the hammer and the trigger guard of the pistol.

Defense counsel asked Humphrey about the evidence and whether or not he made a report detailing his actions at the storage shed on September 15, 1995.

Humphrey replied that no report had been prepared and that he was testifying solely from memory.

Ralph Harp, another FBI agent, testified that he worked with Mr. Humphrey and that he logged in 36 pieces of evidence taken from the storage shed on Billy Allen's property. Nick Fatta, special agent with the Federal Bureau of Alcohol, Tobacco, and Firearms, testified that he was asked by the FBI agents in this case to trace the records of the .45 pistol. Fatta's investigation revealed that the owner was Hilton Crawford and that Hilton purchased the gun at a Houston sporting goods store in 1988.

Gary Capo, the man who had been at Billy Allen's storage building on the morning of September 13, 1995, testified next. He said he knew Billy Allen and just happened to be driving by the storage buildings and saw Allen mowing the lawn. He stopped and the two chatted. He also said that between 8:15 a.m. and 8:30 a.m. Hilton Crawford pulled up in his car. Capo identified the vehicle as a Chrysler.

"How would you describe Hilton that morning?"

"He was not his normal self," Capo stated. "There was something there." Capo could not put his finger on it, but he felt that Hilton had acted strangely.

Elizabeth Schaeffer's father, John, followed Capo. He testified that Connie Crawford, his next-door neighbor, called him at their residence several times in the early morning hours of September 13. The first call from Connie took place around midnight. Schaeffer stated that Connie asked if McKay was at their house. He thought the question was very odd, given the late hour. Connie also said that two different men had just called and said that they were helping the Everetts in trying to find McKay. She said McKay was missing and she thought that Elizabeth might know where he was. Schaeffer said that his wife, who was also named Connie, awoke Elizabeth and asked her if she knew where McKay was or had gone. They hung up. Schaeffer testified that Connie Crawford and Connie Schaeffer talked on the phone a short time later and Connie Crawford said that McKay had been kidnapped.

During another call, he asked Connie where Hilton was, and she responded by saying that Hilton was on a trip to Lufkin. He was supposed to be going on to Beaumont or Lake Charles.

"Then what happened?"

Schaeffer told the court that around 4:30 a.m. the FBI appeared at their home and wanted to talk with Elizabeth.

Schaeffer also testified that he had talked to Nancy Kahn, the neighbor who lived across the street from the Everetts, around 12:30 a.m. and that she told him about the gold-colored Chrysler that her husband had seen entering and exiting the Everetts' residence on the evening of September 12. She also told him about the Crown Motors sticker on the back of the car.

"Did these facts jar your memory as to who might have a car similar to that?"

Schaeffer said yes, that he remembered telling his wife that Hilton Crawford owned a car like that.

The neighbor continued, telling the jury that Wednesday, September 13, Crawford came over to his house around 11 a.m. after he returned from his trip.

"How did he appear to you?"

Schaeffer said that Hilton seemed somewhat reserved, quieter than normal, but showed no worry or concern when told that McKay Everett was missing. He acted, Schaffer said, like the whole situation was no big deal.

"How do you know he was close to McKay Everett?"

Schaeffer said he knew this because Crawford would talk about McKay. He would also tell Elizabeth, Schaeffer's daughter and McKay's school chum, to come along with him whenever he was going over to the Everetts' house. Schaeffer also testified that one time Hilton told Elizabeth that McKay would "be a good catch" because he was rich.

"So you knew that McKay Everett and Hilton Crawford were friends?"

Again Schaeffer replied that the two were very good friends. In fact, he described them as close friends.

Next, Paula Trull, office manager for a Chrysler-Plymouth dealer in Houston, testified that Connie Crawford had purchased a Chrysler LHS there in 1994. She also stated that the LHS had a Crown symbol on the trunk. When Defense Counsel asked Trull if she had, in fact, seen the actual car purchased by Connie Crawford, she replied, "No."

Additional, but central, testimony about Hilton's Chrysler LHS was obtained from Billie Wisham, an auto service consultant at Demontrond Auto Country, located in Conroe. Wisham logged in auto information from customers who brought cars into the dealership for service. She testified that she knew Hilton Crawford because he brought his LHS to the shop for service.

The prosecution asked, "On September 13, 1995, did Mr. Hilton Crawford call you?"

Wisham nodded and stated that Crawford called near lunch-time on the 13th. She said that he wanted to replace his trunk mat because it was wet. Crawford told her that the car was on a lease and that he wanted to replace the mat before he turned the car back in. She told Crawford that she would obtain a price for him. She also said that Crawford wanted her to remember that he threw the wet mat away. He ended the conversation by telling her that he would call back.

Hilton's attorney wanted to know what kind of customer Hilton was. Wisham told the court that Crawford was a good customer and tipped her when she took care of the LHS.

Jeremy Swaney, who worked in the parts department at Demontrond Auto Country, testified that around 1:30 p.m. on September 13, 1995, an unknown caller asked him how to remove an emblem from a vehicle. The caller said it was a Crown Motors emblem. Swaney told the caller to use a chemical called Acryosole to remove the emblem.

"Was that an unusual call for you?"

Swaney replied that it was the only call like that he had ever received. Swaney also reported that the caller's voice sounded like an older man—the voice was rough-sounding and cracked when the caller spoke. When Defense Counsel asked Swaney if he knew who had made the call, however, the witness said that he did not.

Swaney was the last witness in day three of the trial. At the conclusion of his testimony, the jury now had the following informa-tion: Crawford was at a hotel in Beaumont, Texas, in the early-morning hours of September 13, 1995; he sought to store some personal items, including a .45 handgun, in a storage building; the handgun had bloodstains on it; Crawford removed a bloodstained trunk lining from his LHS on September 13; the Crawfords owned a 1994 Chrysler LHS; someone called a Conroe auto dealership and asked how to remove a Crown emblem from an auto. In most events in his life Hilton Crawford had been the lead actor; in this trial, however, as he watched the evidence pile up against him, all that he could do was to watch nervously. Like most puzzle solvers, the prosecutor, through this testimony, had now filled in the border before the last pieces were put in place.

Gale Vohs, a security guard at the Louisiana Pacific Plant in Lufkin, began the testimony on day four of the trial. He was employed by Security Guard Service of Houston, and his supervisor was Hilton Crawford.

The prosecutor: "Did Mr. Crawford make periodic visits to your plant?"

The security guard testified that Crawford rarely came by for visits but that he brought by the employees' pay checks. Vohs went on to say that Crawford called him on September 14, 1995, around 11:00 a.m. Vohs said that Hilton informed him about McKay's kidnapping and that investigators were looking at all vehicles that were similar to his. At this point, Vohs testified that Hilton told him that he had been at the Lufkin plant Tuesday evening around 8:00 p.m. observing the security officers to see how they were doing their jobs.

"Were you on duty at that time?"

Vohs informed the court that he had not been on duty that day.

"What happened next?"

"He asked me," Vohs told the jury, "if I would verify that he was there and he asked if I had a problem with that and I said, 'Yes sir, I don't doubt that you were here if you say so, but I will not state that you were here if I did not see you here.'" Hilton said that he understood and hung up.

Karen Dominy, another security guard at the Louisiana Pacific plant, testified next. She told the court that she had agreed to the FBI's request to monitor and tape record any phone conversations that she might receive. The FBI told Dominy about the kidnapping and suggested that the perpetrator might contact her to use her as an alibi witness. She testified that on the evening of September 14, 1995, she received a phone call from Hilton Crawford. She talked to him three times that day. She said Crawford called her at work and "asked if I could do a favor for him."

"What favor was that?"

"Well," she replied, "he said if anyone called wanting to know if he had been there the night before, to tell them that he had been there at about 9:15 p.m." Crawford called again and told her not to forget that he had been at the plant Tuesday evening, September 12, 1995, around 9:15. During this call, Crawford told her about McKay's kidnapping. On the evening of the 14th, Dominy testified Crawford called her and the conversation was recorded. She informed Crawford that the FBI had contacted her and were coming to talk to her.

Victoria Hale, an FBI agent, testified next. She said that she arrived at Hilton Crawford's Conroe residence around 12:30 p.m. She said that Hilton had invited her and another agent into his house. She described Crawford as cordial and friendly, and he provided them with information about Amway, his business trip to Beaumont, and his relationship with the Everetts. They left soon afterward.

"When did you see Crawford next?"

Hale replied that she saw Crawford later that afternoon when they picked him up and took him to the location of the Chrysler LHS, which was at the elementary school where Connie taught in Conroe. The car was located and impounded.

Hale told the court that she next saw Hilton on the morning of September 15, when they arrested him at his residence. She testified that on the 15th, while under arrest, Crawford first recounted his story to the FBI about having an accomplice, R.L. Remington. She also described Hilton's emotional state at the time of arrest as "distraught."

Next, Marvin Keller, President of Security Guard Services, testified that Crawford was a regional manager for his company. He took care of all the company's accounts in East Texas. Keller said that he and Hilton had known each other since 1979 and that Hilton came to work for him in April of 1992. He said Crawford made about $54,000 a year and had a company car.

"Had you noticed anything about Mr. Crawford's demeanor in the weeks before September 12, 1995?"

Keller responded that Hilton had high blood pressure and was worried a little about his financial situation because he filed "Chapter Seven." "Hilton," Keller said, "told me he was in a bind."

"Can you describe the kind of car that was leased by Mr. Crawford that your company paid for?"

Keller told the court that it was a gold 1994 Chrysler LHS.

David Friday, who followed Marvin Keller, told the jury that he worked at One Price Cleaners in Conroe. He testified that while at work on September 13, 1995, Hilton Crawford brought in a shirt and a pair of pants in the late morning. Friday said that he identified himself as "Lewis Crawford."

"Did you notice anything unusual about the clothes?"

Friday replied, "The garments felt like, if you've been to the beach, they felt like a salt spray, like a sticky salt or something on them." He also said the garments appeared to be dirty.

"Would you tell the jury how Mr. Crawford appeared at the time he brought the clothing in?"

Friday said Crawford seemed tired and his eyes were very puffy. He also said that Crawford was uncommunicative. Friday said that they placed the soiled garments in a labeled bag and sent the bag to the back of the store.

Betty Grantham, another employee at the cleaners, testified that she picked up the bag of clothes tagged with the name Crawford and dumped them on the counter. She said that the clothes were "dirty and sticky, and wet." Grantham told the court that she did not really want to touch them because she didn't know where they had been. The clothes were then cleaned and she hung them on a hanger.

"Did you notice anything about the shirt itself?"

"Yes," she said. "I went over and raised up the plastic and noticed what looked like blood on the front of the shirt."

Defense counsel attempted to undermine Grantham's testimony by asking her if she saw Crawford drop off the clothing, to which she replied, "No."

Following the testimony of the employees of One Price Cleaners, the District Attorney returned to the focus of the trial, Hilton Crawford. Robert Lee, an agent with the FBI, testified about his meeting with Crawford on September 14. Lee and Agent Hale interviewed Hilton at his office in Houston sometime before lunch.

"Did you notice anything in particular about his demeanor when you and Ms. Hale arrived and asked to speak with him?"

Like most good law enforcement investigators, Lee had read Crawford's body for any clue that he might be apprehensive. "When we first arrived to talk to him," Lee said, "he appeared to be real nervous. His hands were shaking, and he just appeared real nervous when we first got there." Lee told the court that Crawford took a phone call, which briefly interrupted the interview. The agents then asked Hilton about his whereabouts on September 12, 1995.

Lee reported Hilton's remembrances to the court. He said Crawford told him that he waited on a security guard employee at his house to go with him to the 8:00 p.m. Amway meeting. The employee never showed up, so he decided to leave Conroe on business. Crawford told the agents that he left his residence at 8:10 p.m. and drove to Lufkin to meet a security guard at the Louisiana Pacific plant. He met with the guard for a short time and then left Lufkin around 9:00 p.m. and drove on to Jasper. He arrived there around 10:45 p.m. He stayed in Jasper until 11:30 p.m. and then drove to Beaumont. He arrived in Beaumont around 1:30 a.m. and ate at a Waffle House and then checked into a Best Western hotel around 2:00 a.m.

Lee testified that at this point Crawford showed him the credit card receipt, or the paid room bill. He then continued with his story, Lee said, and told them that he called his wife around 6:00 a.m. and she told him that McKay Everett had been kidnapped. He said his wife asked him to call the Kahns to see if they could assist in any way. Crawford also said that he called Billy Allen around 7 a.m.

Agent Lee said Hilton next told them that he left the hotel and went to Silsbee to meet the plant manager for Louisiana Pacific. Crawford said the plant manager was unavailable, so he met with an assistant. Lee testified that he and Agent Hale asked Hilton to provide the contact information for the people he allegedly met with on his trip. Lee said that Crawford was evasive in this regard but said that he would provide necessary information at some point. He then told the two agents he arrived home around 12:15 p.m.

The interview then turned to Hilton's relationship with McKay. Lee told the court that Hilton told them that he had been to the Everetts' house on many occasions and that McKay had been over to his house on several occasions. He mentioned that McKay's girlfriend lived next door to him. He felt that he knew McKay well enough that if he had gone to the Everetts' residence by himself when Mr. and Mrs. Everett weren't there, McKay would have admitted him into the house. He also believed that McKay would have gotten in the car and gone somewhere with him if he had asked him to do so. Lee said that he and Agent Hale left and reported the results of this interview to their command post.

"Did you see Mr. Crawford again that day?"

Agent Lee replied that he saw Hilton later that afternoon when he brought his LHS to the Conroe FBI office. The agents examined the car in the parking lot.

"Did you notice anything peculiar about it?"

Lee replied matter-of-factly, "Yes, we did. We went to the back of the car and on the trunk, in the left-hand corner, there was a partial sticker we could read: *Crown Motors*. We could see that the sticker had been peeled off. I touched the trunk where the glue had been and it was still very tacky. There were some scrape marks in the paint where the sticker had been peeled off, no rust had formed, and no road grime had stuck to the glue residue that was still there. We noticed that the car was very clean and the tires were very shiny." The agent told the court that the car was then impounded. The agents also looked inside at the trunk.

Lee testified that Crawford, without prompting, told them why the lining was missing. He said the lining had gotten wet and that a worker at Demontrond Auto instructed him to take the lining out and let it dry. Crawford also told them that the lining smelled bad, so he threw it away.

"Then what happened?"

Lee told the court that on September 15, 1995, he and a team of law enforcement officers arrested Crawford at his residence around 6:30 a.m. Lee said, "We took him to the dining room and read him his rights. He stated that he understood his rights and he waived them."

Lee's testimony was critical—he put most of the pieces of the puzzle together. Prior to Lee, the witnesses had each contributed to the picture, dropping their puzzle pieces on the table one by one. The frame was first assembled, then the interior, and the picture slowly came into focus. Only a few other pieces, typically those with odd or jagged edges, remained on the table. Putting them together would not be difficult.

Defense counsel tried to counter Lee's testimony by suggesting that Hilton's shaking hands were not an unusual response by someone confronted by the FBI.

One of the missing pieces of the puzzle involved the ransom call. The testimony of FBI agent Lloyd Dias, began to fill in this gap in the picture. Dias told the court that his role in the case was to examine Crawford's cellular phone records. He said, "On September 12, three calls from his mobile phone were placed to a particular number, and these calls were placed near the time that we thought McKay Everett had been abducted. We ran the number to see who it belonged to, and that person was Irene Flores, who lived in Houston."

"Did you talk with Irene Flores?"

Dias said, "Two other agents, a Montgomery County deputy, and I talked to her for approximately three hours on September 15. At first she was evasive, but then revealed she made the ransom call." Dias also told the court that after his interview with Flores, he contacted other FBI agents, who proceeded to obtain an arrest warrant for Crawford. Dias was part of the arrest team that took Hilton into custody.

Special agent Dias was also present on September 14, when Crawford's' LHS was examined by agents at the Conroe FBI office.

"Did you notice anything unusual about the lip of the rim of the trunk, itself?"

"Yes, sir, the weather stripping was depressed, or indented. It looked like something was pried in between the top of the trunk and the weather stripping to make an indent like that. It was done from inside the trunk. The weather stripping was pried downward."

And then the obvious but most chilling question: "As if someone was attempting to get out?"

Dias replied, "Yes, sir."

From the beginning of the trial until this very moment, Paulette knew that there would be testimony about McKay in the trunk. She knew it would come and had even asked the District Attorney to alert her to this testimony so she could exit the courtroom. No warning came. The evidence revealed that McKay had been trying to claw his way out of the trunk. Her frightened child had been fighting for his life.

At hearing Dias' reply, Paulette told herself, "Oh my God, this is it, this is about McKay being held captive in the trunk of a car and fighting for his life!" She had tried hard to be a good victim, to be quiet, to wear a poker face in spite of any emotional testimony. But that poker face evaporated as the feelings of hurt and horror bubbled up in her like lava. She could not contain herself. Who could?

Paulette began to make squeaking sounds, and she told herself, "*Stop it, stop it!*" It was no use. She began to scream hysterically. She screamed and screamed and looked at Hilton. As if in slow motion, Crawford turned his head and looked at Paulette.

The judge began immediately pounding his gavel and yelled, "Order in the court!" He yelled it over and over. It looked like a scene from a movie. The pounding and screaming continued for several minutes. The jury was removed from the courtroom, along with Hilton.

Paulette's mother acted as if she might faint. Carl offered assistance to his overcome wife. The entire courtroom was cleared while Paulette collected herself. She was frozen in her chair. After a few minutes she walked out of the courtroom, and Carl drove her home. In the car Paulette told herself, "You know something? I feel better."

After the Everetts left, the courtroom participants filed back in and the trial resumed. Defense Counsel asked for a mistrial but was denied. The judge instructed the jury to disregard the episode and stay true to their role—to consider the presented evidence only. Paulette was admonished that should any future outburst occur, she and Carl would be barred from the courtroom. The court's message was clear: *It is a privilege for you to be here, so you'd better sit still and keep your mouths shut.* Victims were to be seen and not heard. Good victims were bystanders.

Trial testimony commenced at 9:00 a.m. on July 12. Three law enforcement officials testified about various pieces of evidence, including a pager, paint thinner, and bug and tar cleanser found in Hilton's possession.

Then came dramatic testimony. Guy Williams, Sheriff of Montgomery County, testified that on the morning of September 16, 1995, Hilton Crawford, who was confined in the Montgomery County Jail, told him that Samuel McKay Everett was dead.

"Did he tell you where McKay Everett was?"

"Yes, sir," replied Williams. He testified further: "Hilton was upset. He was shaking real bad. His voice was cracking."

The sheriff also said that Crawford provided them with a rough map on Saturday night (September 16) that described the location where McKay's body could be found.

"Describe for the jury, please, where Crawford said the body of McKay Everett was located."

Williams said that the map directed officials to a place called Whiskey Bay, located in Louisiana.

"Crawford advised us," said Williams, "to go out Interstate 10, eastbound, to Whiskey Bay and exit off the highway, go underneath the freeway, go back down onto a shell-type road, to go down a little bit, there was a driveway going to the area where there was a little building to the right. Left of the building about thirty feet in the bushes is where we could find McKay Everett's body." On this day, Hilton's memory had been pretty clear.

Crawford's defense attorney asked Williams, "Did he appear glad to be talking?"

Williams told the court, "Yeah." The sheriff also stated that Crawford was helpful in describing different landmarks along the route to McKay's body.

Two law enforcement officers—one from Iberville Parish and one from St. Martin Parish—had found McKay's body in some high weeds during the early morning hours of September 17. The location of the body was in accordance with the directions and hand-drawn map provided by Crawford. Four days after McKay went missing, in the hot and humid conditions of the Atchafalaya swampland, law enforcement officials had recovered the horribly decomposed body of the twelve-year-old boy. It was time for McKay to come home.

Chapter 6

A Constellation of Blood

The first several days of the trial, I sat there and listened to the witnesses tell the jury their stories. Everything seemed so obvious. The testimony clearly pointed to Hilton. A complete stranger who walked into court and heard the same things I did would come to the same conclusion. I was sure of it. I listened closely to the witnesses, trying to hear anything that might in any way cast doubt on Hilton's guilt. I heard nothing that could in any way let that monster off the hook. I knew he did it. But I also knew that the jury needed hard facts. When I heard the witnesses talk about guns, bullets, and my child's blood and poor body and what he went through, I thought I would die right there in that courtroom. It was awful, and nothing—I mean nothing—prepared me for that. I thought I was going to collapse when I heard what happened to McKay in terms of the hard evidence. Hearing that testimony just about killed me. I knew that it was necessary to nail Hilton's coffin shut, but I cannot tell you what it was like for me to hear it. It was absolutely gut-wrenching.

The bulk of the testimony, to this point, had been witness accounts of Crawford's movements, his background, and details surrounding the night of September 12, 1995. Some physical evidence—phone records and gas receipts and the make and color of Hilton's car—had been introduced. These latter pieces of evidence were crucial in the case against Crawford. The evidence was indeed piling up against him. However, evidence was still required that placed Hilton at the scene of the crime.

The jury had to see that Crawford was at the swamp scene. It was also important that they hear and understand how McKay Everett died, how the wicked blows crushed his skull, how the gunshot tore his body apart, and how his poor damaged remains were ravaged by insects, moist soil, animals, and the heat and foul air of Whiskey Bay. It was time, way past time, that the jury saw hard evidence. Hilton Crawford—Uncle Hilty—was about to be unmasked.

Sheriff Williams from Montgomery County retook the witness stand on July 15, 1996, day six of the trial. Williams testified that as late as September 15, 1995—four days after the kidnapping—authorities still held out hope that McKay would be found alive.

Williams told the court that he and two FBI agents talked to Hilton around 9:30 p.m. on Saturday, September 16. Williams said, "We told Crawford our priority at this time was the recovery of McKay, to which he replied, 'He's dead.' We then asked where the body could be recovered and he said, 'I can tell you.' Crawford was shaking real bad and he couldn't hold a pen. So we asked him to give us directions to where McKay's body was at."

Williams continued his story: "Hilton then gave the directions as follows: 'Go east on Interstate 10 past Lafayette, Louisiana, to a place called Whiskey Bay. Exit the freeway and go back under it to the other side.' He said the road was unpaved and there would be a shell-type road leading up to an iron gate. He said when looking at the gate you could see something that looked like a wooden shed or something like a shed. He said McKay's body was off to the left in some grass about—and he motioned—approximately two to three feet high. He said McKay's body was covered with some type of brush approximately 30 feet off the road. He advised that McKay had been shot at the location. He then began to settle down somewhat, so for clarification we gave him a pen and he sketched a crude map of the exit, the road, and the area on Special Agent Jones' notepad."

Williams said following the revelation, the FBI exited the interview room and immediately telephoned other federal agents in Lafayette to tell them to retrieve McKay's body.

McKay's remains were found in the early morning hours of September 17, 1995. Williams told the court that he and a minister drove to the Everett residence and informed them that McKay was dead.

Williams testified that Hilton denied killing McKay. He said that Crawford pinned the actual murder on a man named R.L. Remington. He also said that Crawford did not want to do prison time in Louisiana.

Blair Favaron, captain and crime scene investigator for the Iberville Parish Sheriff's Office, testified that around 1:45 a.m. on September 17, 1995, he received a telephone call about where to find a body at the Whiskey Bay exit along I-10. Favaron testified that the highway exit was easy to find but there was no lighting in the area, either on I-10 or the Louisiana highways that intersect I-10. In other words, the Whiskey Bay exit was accessible and dark, very dark at night.

"Have there been few or many occasions where law enforcement officials have discovered bodies dumped in this low area?" asked the prosecution.

The veteran crime scene investigator replied, "Unfortunately, yes—many." Favaron told the jury that when he arrived at the scene on September 17, 1995, there were FBI agents and deputies securing the area. He stated that other investigators took a number of photographs of the crime scene where McKay's body was found. He also assisted a crime scene investigator from the Louisiana Department of Public Safety in videotaping the entire crime scene. The video was shown to the jury over the objections of Hilton's attorneys. The weeds leading to the body were bent over in one direction. Favaron testified that bent weeds were a "drag path," or that someone had dragged McKay's body to a location in the weeds and left him there. The area where the body was found was covered in dense underbrush. After the videotape was made, Favaron said, McKay's body was removed and brought to a local morgue.

The prosecutor asked, "Was the victim wearing any kind of shirt at all?"

Favaron testified that McKay did have a shirt on but that it had been pulled up around his midsection.

"Why was it pulled up?"

"It was apparent to me," Favaron said, "that the individual had been drug by the legs, by the feet."

In short, the jury was made aware that McKay was unconscious, or already dead, when he was dragged by his feet on his back, or stomach, to the final spot in the weeds. Favaron also said that after searching the area for three days with a metal detector, their team found two .45 shell casings.

As a result of these crucial discoveries, the crime scene investigator cordoned off the area in a grid to find the spent bullets that belonged to the cartridges. How deep would a bullet penetrate the swampy soil? A field test was needed to answer this question. The team took a ten-millimeter handgun—which was all they had with them that approximated a .45—and at a nearby location fired a bullet into the ground. The bullet went down around six inches. The team returned to the site where McKay's body was found and they began digging about two or three feet deep. They put shovels of swampy soil into wheelbarrows and passed the soil over wire screens.

The investigators resembled archeologists searching for a bit of jaw bone, a tooth, a finger, a piece of skull, or any tidbit that might lead to the fabled missing link. Their efforts were rewarded. They found the spent bullet, photographed it, and placed the important piece of evidence in a bag. The investigators had located their missing link, which to them was a discovery of a lifetime. It required some effort, but Whiskey Bay was slowly giving up its secrets, as if the collective voices of all the murder victims who had been dumped in the swamp were saying, "Not here. No, not here—you can't leave a child here." The voices in the swamp begged for justice. Indeed, the swamp wanted no part of this foul deed and eagerly surrendered the little treasures hidden beneath its rotting soil needed to implicate Hilton. For once in its secret history, Whiskey Bay, a bone yard, was willing to help solve a crime.

The physical evidence was a key piece of the overall puzzle. Randy Sillivan, a firearms examiner with thirty years of experience with the Montgomery County Sheriff's Department, testified that the two shells and spent bullet found at Whiskey Bay were from a .45 pistol. Sillivan test-fired Hilton's .45 and compared the shell markings from Hilton's gun with those found on the shells in Louisiana. He did the same with the bullets as well. He told the jury that when a firearm was fired, the bullet passed down the barrel and picked up tool markings and striations along the way. The little markings on the bullet were unique, like fingerprints. The little marks on the spent bullet recovered from Whiskey Bay did not lie. Sillivan also examined the two spent shells, looking for tool marks. Marks on the cartridges from the firing pin were also unique identifiers.

From Sillivan's test came a single conclusion: The spent cartridges and bullet were fired from one pistol, labeled "States exhibit n. 50." It was the same gun that Billy Allen had seen among the personal items that Hilton Crawford sought to store at Allen's storage business and the same pistol that he had bought at a sporting goods store in Houston.

"What brand of ammunition were the bullets?"

Sillivan told the court that the manufacturer of the cartridges was a company called Remington-Peters.

Next, James Freeman, the coroner of Iberville Parish, testified about the cause of McKay's death. Freeman had been a physician and surgeon since 1958, and in his position as coroner his job was to investigate deaths, especially suspicious ones. He was also trained in pathology, or the study of disease and death. Freeman was a veteran of autopsies, having performed about 2,800 in his career. The doctor testified that on September 18, 1995, at 10 a.m., he began a post-mortem examination and autopsy on the body of McKay Everett.

"Can you describe the general condition of the body at the time you started the autopsy?"

Freeman testified that McKay's body was "in an advanced state of decomposition, putrefaction, and had been scavenged by both insects and carnivorous animals, flesh-eating animals, and was laden with probably a million or more maggots." This information caused a collective lump in the throat of the audience. It was difficult to listen to Freeman talk so matter-of-factly about the condition of the boy's body.

"What was the cause of death?"

Freeman said his investigation found that the body had a bullet wound in the back right portion of the head. There were also injuries to the skull over the right temple area and over the left eye socket. Freeman told the court that the gunshot would have caused instantaneous death and that the injury to the boy's right temple, by a round-ended instrument, could also have caused his death as some of the bones were pushed inward toward the brain. The injury to McKay's left eye would have been painful, but it was not a deathblow. Freeman also told the court that the injury over the eye would have cut the skin and that blood would have freely flowed. Freeman found no ligature marks on McKay's hands or feet, meaning that he had not been bound. The cause of death was a gunshot and/or blunt trauma near the back of the right head area.

Following Freeman was Kim Colomb, a forensic scientist with the Louisiana State Police Crime Lab. She testified that, during her examination of the crime scene, she picked up two empty Bud Light beer cans and one empty Marlboro Lights "100" cigarette pack.

"Why did you do that?"

Colomb told the court that she had picked items up to search for fingerprints. She found no prints on the empty beer cans but found one print on the cigarette pack and compared the print to one on a fingerprint card. The print had not belonged to Hilton Crawford.

By the conclusion of day six, the jury had been presented with critical pieces of information that linked Hilton to the kidnapping and murder of McKay Everett. The jury learned that the map drawn by Crawford leading authorities to McKay's remains was extremely accurate, that law enforcement officials found spent shell casings and a bullet from a .45 handgun, that the shell casings and bullet found at the Whiskey Bay crime scene were fired from Crawford's pistol, and that the cause of the death was a gunshot wound to the back of McKay's head.

The prosecution had pieced together the facts surrounding the abduction and murder of McKay Everett. The jury had seen important physical evidence, such as the gun linking Hilton to the crime scene. This part of the case was very clear.

Defense attorneys for Hilton tried as best they could to cast doubt on the integrity of the crime scene and the gathering of the evidence. Their efforts, however, were increasingly feeble.

On July 16, 1996, the prosecution presented additional physical evidence about the crime: the physical deterioration of McKay's remains and the wounds suffered by the boy. The presentation of this kind of evidence, like the first cut on a cadaver, was not for the squeamish. Day seven of the trial was brutal and was most horrifying for Paulette.

The first witness on this day was Professor Chester Meek, an entomologist at Louisiana State University. Meek was no ordinary professor of critters, or bug detector. He was a forensic entomologist, someone who studies insects and the general climate of the area associated with decaying cadavers and carcasses. When McKay's remains were found, they were heavily laden with insects and their eggs, and Meek's job was to examine what kinds of insects had invaded McKay's body. The prosecution also offered this testimony to shed light on the time of death.

The prosecutor asked Professor Meek if McKay's body "wound up at the particular location, certainly no later than sunrise on the 13th?" Meek examined the climate at the time and knew all about the insects of the Whiskey Bay area, and he testified that McKay's body had been placed in the swamp sometime between midnight, September 12, and sunrise, September 13. While graphic, Meek's testimony placed important parameters around the time of death.

Next Butch Emmons, a crime scene investigator with the Montgomery County Sheriff's Department, testified that on September 14, he assisted two of his colleagues and two FBI agents in processing Hilton Crawford's vehicle. The vehicle was searched in a Sheriff's Department building. Emmons stated that he found the vehicle to be exceptionally clean. The tires, he noted, were very shiny from a recent detailing. Emmons said that the tires on the car had been recently changed because they were not the Goodyear Double Eagles that came on the car from the factory. It was odd that all four tires should have been replaced on a new car. On the outside, Emmons saw that someone had tried to remove the *Crown Motors* dealership sticker.

Emmons testified that the team turned their attention to the trunk. Opening it, they found that all of the inner carpet and lining had been removed, including the carpet from the underside of the trunk lid. The team thought that this was strange, given the fact that the LHS was relatively new. Emmons said they removed several hairs and fibers from the trunk by hand. But they were after more than fibers. They were on the trail of blood.

Emmons told the court that the team removed the spare tire and jack. They searched the empty trunk for blood, but saw none. Using a spray bottle, they misted the trunk area with luminol, a "wonder chemical" used in finding hard-to-see or invisible blood evidence.

Luminol reacts specifically to hemoglobin, an oxygen-carrying protein in red blood cells. This chemical can detect even trace amounts of blood that could be many years old. Even though Hilton had torn out the trunk lining and meticulously cleaned his car, a mist of luminol would reveal any blood.

Emmons knew where to look, and he found little pockets of blood. The luminol-exposed blood spots looked like twinkling stars on a clear summer night. They found a constellation of blood in the trunk. Emmons also located blood inside the trunk around several areas where the rubber seal had been pried or loosened. And he found bloodstains on the floor of the trunk in the spare-tire well. The stains were removed for further analysis.

Emmons knew the habits of blood, how it flies and spatters, how it flows, how it pools, and how it dries. If he thought blood was in the trunk, he was going to find it. He was like an old-time Western sheriff reading tracks and signs on the ground in search of rustlers and renegades. Emmons lay on his back inside the trunk and noticed low- and medium-velocity blood spatters around the metal area by the car's speakers, concentrated on the driver's side. The spatters were tiny, about the diameter of a toothpick, but were crucial pieces to finishing the puzzle. The trunk, like the swamp, was giving up its secrets. They took dozens of photographs of the car and trunk. It took more than a week to examine the entire car and collect the necessary evidence.

Despite Hilton's efforts, the little damned spots, like those on Lady Macbeth's hands, would not be erased. Touched by the modern mist luminol, they glowed.

To further corroborate McKay's cause of death, Emmons told the court that the victim's remains were forwarded to Daniel Glassman, a forensic anthropologist in San Marcos, Texas. Based on Glassman's report, Emmons told the court that McKay suffered a blunt trauma injury to the area above his nose and from one to three blows to the right side of his head. McKay had also been shot twice, once in the neck and once in the chest.

The jurors heard the Louisiana coroner mention one bullet, whereas the Texas specialist reported two bullet wounds. Both experts, however, agreed about the death blows to the right side of McKay's head.

Mary Manheim, Director of Forensic Anthropology at Louisiana State University, testified about the extent of injuries to McKay's skull: a bullet wound eerily reminiscent of the one found on the back of John F. Kennedy's head in 1964, as well as blunt-force trauma injuries. She concluded that he had been hit at least two times on the head.

This trial day was very long, not in seconds or minutes, but in the complexities of the physical evidence. One had to remain attentive to understand how the physical evidence, layer upon layer, factored in the case and pinned the crime on Crawford. The jury heard that McKay's body had been placed on the ground at Whiskey Bay sometime between midnight September 12 and dawn on the 13th, that bloodstains had been found inside the gold LHS cab and trunk, and that McKay had suffered horrible injuries. Only a few loose ends needed tying up.

DNA experts from the Texas Department of Public Safety's crime lab testified that samples of blood from Hilton's clothes, the gun, the rubber seal from inside the gold LHS, the armrest, and the inside of the trunk had been examined. Their conclusions confirmed the findings of the Louisiana investigators.

Specimens from these five stains had been forwarded to Meghan Clement, Assistant Director of the Forensic Identity Testing Division at Laboratory Corporation of American Holdings, in North Carolina. She testified that the bloodstains found on Hilton's shirt and inside the trunk had come from McKay Everett.

The prosecutor asked Clement: "What was the probability that Carl and Paulette Everett were the parents of the donor of these bloodstains you examined?"

She replied, "99.9%."

The prosecutor, seeking more precision, asked her: "In other words, 99.9 percent of the time, Carl and Paulette Everett would be the natural parents of the donor of the DNA extracts taken from the shirt and from the trunk?"

Again, Clement told the jury in simple language, "Basically, what it states is that the probability that they are the parents is 99.9 percent."

Defense counsel tried as best they could to suggest that being 99.9 % sure was still not 100%. The forensic identity expert agreed, but the percentage made no difference. McKay's blood had now been firmly established as being inside the trunk and on Crawford's shirt.

At the close of this phase of the trial, the jury was exposed to and asked to consider important pieces of physical evidence. The pieces of physical evidence had to be considered in their totality. Looking at the midnight sky, one sees millions of stars, dots that seem unconnected. But careful examination of the stars reveals patterns. Some stars hang together to form shapes or constellations that look like humans or animals. The blood spatters in the McKay Everett murder trial initially seemed like unrelated stars, but the investigators connected the spatters and made them reveal their pattern. The constellation of blood in the car represented McKay Everett. No matter how hard Hilton had tried to erase the evidence, the blood stayed inside the trunk, and modern technology had found it out. Lady Macbeth and Hilton Crawford, though separated by the centuries, had dirty hands.

Chapter 7

Motive and Decision

I listened to every word the witnesses said, but few gave me any indication as to why Hilton did what he did. Why did he do this? I wanted him to get up on that stand like a man and tell me why, just tell me why he did this. I really wanted him to look me in the eyes and tell me straight. I knew he killed McKay, and I wanted those people on the jury to understand what was in his head. I knew why he did it. He did it because of gambling. A lousy gambling habit was responsible for him killing McKay. He took my baby away from me because he gambled and got in over his head. He took my baby away from me because he could not control his own self. There was no way he could have ever gotten away with it. Carl and I knew Hilton was a gambler, but I never thought he would kill over it. I guessed wrong.

The average *who done it* on television begins with a horrible crime and then, during the next sixty minutes, the tension builds as investigators unlock various clues to the mystery. Potential suspects are eliminated along the way until the real perpetrator is finally uncovered. All the evidence lies squarely at the feet of the offender.

One of the most compelling questions in any television or big-screen crime drama is the motive for the crime. Viewers want to know why the accused *did it*, and cases are typically not resolved without a segment devoted to motive. In real-world criminal trials, however, motive is a secondary issue. In any state's criminal statutes, motive is not an element in a felony act. Jealousy, for example, is not one of the elements that constitute murder. Prosecutors may inject motive as a backdrop or a reason for the crime, and motive may help the jury assemble the pieces of evidence around some plausible explanation for the crime. But motive is not a necessary condition for a conviction, and a prosecutor does not have to prove it in order to make a case.

At this point in the trial, Crawford's reasons were still fuzzy. The case facts were ghastly, almost beyond comprehension. Here was the defendant, a former police officer, who had beaten and shot to death a twelve-year-old boy, then dragged his body into a weedy swamp and abandoned it there, where it lay for five days, ravaged by insects, carnivorous animals, and the elements. Almost as grotesque was the betrayal of trust. McKay Everett had known his killer fondly as "Uncle Hilty," and Crawford had both personal and professional ties with the Everett parents. He and Carl had been business partners. His wife, Connie, and Paulette had taught first grade together.

Perhaps most inexplicable was the fact that Hilton Crawford did not fit the profile of such a criminal. All the social and psychological research on criminals suggests that crime is a young man's profession. Of those felons imprisoned in our society, the vast majority are non-white males, less than thirty years old, from inner-city areas. Most of these convicted criminals have not graduated from high school and have spotty work records. They often come from dysfunctional families, and many have a history of substance abuse.

Compared to the ordinary American criminal, Crawford was a complete anomaly. To a large degree, he was the exact opposite of any standard criminal profile. He wasn't suffering from an addiction to the bottle or crack cocaine or any kind of narcotic that might have impaired his reasoning power. He was not a victim of society or some maladjusted punk from the mean streets, like Charles Manson or Richard Speck, or some child from nowhere with a chip on his shoulder, eager to kill to prove he is a man. He wasn't some rebel without a cause, or some psychopath like Ted Bundy, who enjoyed hunting and killing humans.

Hilton Crawford was an older white man, with a job, a decent income, a wife and sons, a future, and a nice house with a pool in the suburbs. Most would say that Crawford had it made. What, then, compelled him to commit a senselessly dark act, to murder without a shred of remorse a child he knew well? What was it? Were things really that bad? What could possibly drive a man his age to kidnap and murder? Crawford, a former police officer, certainly knew that kidnapping and murder cases are typically solved. People just don't get away with these crimes. What drove him to roll the dice?

The prosecutor wanted the jury to have answers to these questions. And the jury was all ears when Joe Duhon strode into the courtroom, took the oath, and sat down in the witness stand. Joe Duhon trained race horses in Shreveport, Louisiana. He testified that he had known Hilton for twenty years. In fact, Duhon trained Texas Rode, a horse Crawford owned. The horse raced at Louisiana Downs in Bossier City. This was the same track where Hilton maintained that he met R.L. Remington in 1993. Hilton had trouble paying the horse trainer's fees. Duhon sent Hilton bills but never received payment.

The prosecution asked, "How much did he owe you?"

"Somewhere between $3,500 and $4,500."

"How was he going to get the money?" asked the prosecutor.

Duhon told the court that during a phone conversation, Hilton said that if he could not get the money, he would kill himself or somebody else.

Another horse track friend of Hilton's, J. Herrin, told the court that in August of 1995, a few weeks before McKay's disappearance, Hilton offered him $80,000 to "baby-sit a kid for a few days" in a kidnapping scheme in which the unhurt kid would be returned to the parents. Herrin declined. But he willingly testified about Crawford's bizarre offer, which amounted in sports jargon to "no harm, no foul." Herrin's testimony revealed that Hilton actually believed he could kidnap a child, collect the ransom, and then play golf in the afternoon. The jurors must have been shocked that the one-time deputy sheriff thought it possible to get away with kidnap and murder. Hilton did not look too smart sitting in his chair in front of the jury and in full view of the courtroom audience. It must have been embarrassing.

Following Herrin was Marty Spiller, a real estate agent at the well-to-do Bentwater Resort on Lake Conroe. Prior to the kidnapping, Crawford had gone into Spiller's real estate office and asked to look at houses for sale. Spiller testified that Hilton was especially interested in one house listed at $290,000. Hilton even talked about installing a bar in the home. He was planning on entertaining in the aftermath of the crime.

Marty Spiller was the last witness in the entire drama. He was a fitting finale, as his brief but potent testimony illustrated the real Crawford. The jury heard how Hilton was going to profit personally from the kidnapping and murder of McKay Everett. Hilton, the big operator, had it all planned out. He had even spent the money before he killed for it; he looked pitiful and evil sitting in his chair. The jury heard from Spiller about the calculating and cunning Hilton Crawford.

Throughout the trial Crawford had made his wishes known that he wanted to testify. He wanted his day in court. At the last moment, however, he told the judge that he was not going to testify. The defense rested. They put no witnesses forward and were resigned to the fact that the jury would find Hilton guilty. It was better to argue for Hilton's life than to contest his guilt. The State rested as well and closed with the simple statement that after reviewing the evidence, the jury had no choice but to find Hilton Crawford guilty beyond a reasonable doubt. The defense closed by stating that the prosecution had not clearly established how McKay was taken, or exactly how the boy had been killed, or who else had been involved in the crime. Defense counsel suggested the mysterious R.L. Remington was involved but had never been apprehended and that the real killer was "out there" on the loose.

At 3:30 p.m., on July 19, 1996, the jury retired to deliberate. To deliberate means to act in a purposeful and methodological manner, and one would think that the jury, as in the movies, would review each piece of testimony and debate the issues. After all, a man's life was on the line. But capital trials in the vast majority of cases are like poorly scripted "whodunnits"—most observers know the outcome, from the first scene forward. The case Hilton Crawford vs. The State of Texas was not going to end with a surprise. Everyone in the courtroom knew what the verdict would be. The only issue now on the table was how long it would take the jury to render it.

At 4:51 p.m., scarcely sixty minutes after the jury had retired to deliberate, they notified the court that they had arrived at a verdict. It had taken them a mere sixty minutes to distill eight days of witness testimony, barely one hour to seal Hilton's fate. Members of the jury filed into the courtroom and took their seats.

With the proper decorum and formality expected of his role, the Judge spoke: "Would the foreperson please rise? Ma'am, have you reached a verdict?"

The foreperson, Joy King, spoke on cue, "Yes, sir."

The Judge replied, "Is the verdict unanimous?"

The foreperson stated, "Yes, sir."

The judge then asked her to hand the verdict to the court bailiff, who in turn gave it to the Judge.

The Judge stated, "Mr. Crawford, please rise. Case no. 95-11-01293, the State of Texas vs. Hilton Lewis Crawford. We, the jury, find the defendant, Hilton Lewis Crawford, guilty of capital murder." Each juror was polled about the verdict. And then it was over.

Upon hearing the verdict, Paulette said that she heard McKay's voice speaking in the verdict. She and Carl left the courtroom.

Chapter 8

Life or Death

The trial was an ordeal for me, but I was glad that I had the chance to testify. When the jury came back with that guilty verdict, I was so happy. I was relieved. I was tired, too, but hearing the word "guilty" stated in that courtroom validated everything I knew and what all those witnesses said. It was a great day for McKay. Before the trial, the District Attorney told Carl and me that death penalty trials were different from regular trials. I was not sure what he meant by that. He told us that after the guilt and innocence part, he had to argue before the jury about the proper punishment. He told us that the jury could give Hilton life in prison, but he would argue for the death penalty. More witnesses, more testimony, and more memories, but I wanted to see it through to the end. I had to be there for McKay. How could anyone think that Hilton deserved to live after what he did to McKay?

Death penalty trials in Texas, and those throughout the nation, changed in the 1970s because of Supreme Court rulings. Every capital murder trial now has two phases. In the first of those, the guilt-innocence phase, Hilton was found guilty of capital murder. The second phase involves the assessment of punishment. For Texas capital juries, there are only two possible outcomes to consider: life in prison or death by lethal injection. The trial of Hilton Crawford came down to this final decision. There had never been much doubt about guilt. Hilton's fate was in the hands of twelve of his peers. He was going to be held accountable for his actions. To Paulette, the whole ordeal seemed like a football game. The first half was over and her side was ahead, but they had to keep the pressure on, to stay on the offensive, if they were going to win the second half.

Determining a capital murderer's fate is no easy task. In all probability, the members of the jury in the Crawford case were being asked to make the most serious decision of their lives. However, Texas law provides them with some guidance. In the sentencing phase, the jurors would be asked to answer two specific questions:

1. Whether there was a probability that the defendant would commit criminal acts of violence that would constitute a continuing threat to society; and

2. Whether the defendant actually caused the death of the deceased or did not actually cause the death of the deceased but intended to kill the deceased or another or anticipated that a human life would be taken.

Answering these two questions would determine Hilton's future. If the jury unanimously agreed that the answer to both questions and issues was *yes*, Crawford would receive the death sentence. Issue #2 had essentially been determined in the guilt-innocence phase. The central issue in the "Trial of the Century" was now whether Hilton Crawford was a continuing threat to society. After all, if Hilton were sentenced to life in prison—in 1996, a term of forty years with no conditions for good behavior—he would die behind bars. Since he was already 57, he was a dead man, no matter what the jury decided. The only issue left to decide was when he would die. The State was arguing for a quick exit.

Hilton Crawford was no ordinary murderer—he was a convicted child killer, a man who had betrayed his family friends. Worse yet, he looked like a modern pied piper who had lured a twelve-year-old boy to his death. It was hard to believe that anyone could do such a thing. The jury must have wondered what evidence existed that would mitigate against execution.

The pivotal issue in Texas capital murder trials is whether or not a defendant will be violent in the future. The prosecutor sought the maximum penalty, death, but had to prove that Hilton was a continuing threat to society. The defense, on the other hand, had to show the jury that Hilton was not and would not be a threat to society. In short, the jury was asked to peer into a crystal ball and predict the future.

Predicting whether or not someone will be violent in the future is a messy business. Human behavior is never fully predictable. Who can say with any accuracy what someone will do tomorrow, next month, next year, or five years from now? Ironically, imprisoned killers are often the best-behaved inmates. Even Ted Bundy was a good inmate. Susan Atkins and Patricia Krenwinkel, the whacked-out groupies in the Manson family, were convicted of the Tate-LaBianca murders in 1971 and received life sentences in California. Both emerged from the ashes of their former bizarre lives as killers to become model prisoners. The idea that killers will behave as law-abiding citizens in prison goes against the grain, against what most people might think, and against the idea of future dangerousness.

Current research on murderers and capital murderers, however, supports this idea that killers make pretty good prisoners. In a study of the future dangerousness of Texas capital offenders, researchers examined two groups of murderers—one of them a group of ninety prisoners who had been sent to death row but then for some reason had their sentences overturned on appeal or commuted. These former death-row prisoners entered the general prisoner population. The other group consisted of 107 prisoners convicted of capital murder who had been sentenced to life imprisonment because juries failed to answer "yes" to the "future dangerousness" question during the punishment stage of their trials. The prison and post-prison behavior of the offenders from both groups was examined over the time period of 1974-1988.

The results of this study showed that one former death-row prisoner killed another prisoner, and one "lifer" sexually assaulted another prisoner. However, two-thirds of the prisoners in both groups had never been to solitary confinement, a prison punishment for serious disciplinary infractions. One-fifth of inmates in both groups had no record of any prison rule infraction. In short, eight out of ten prisoners from both groups had not committed serious rule violations and did not constitute a future threat to society. Killers do well in prison, but like Kenneth McDuff, they just cannot handle freedom very well.

The jurors in their decision about the offenders in the first group were wrong most of the time. The vast majority of the prisoners in this group, though labeled a future threat, did not go on to become a threat. In terms of the second group, the jurors were right most of the time when they decided that the offenders were continuing threats to society. In other words, the data indicate that jurors are usually wrong when they make a prediction about future dangerousness, and they are usually right when they decide that a convicted capital murderer is not a threat.

Science aside, the task before the jury was not an easy one. Would they see Hilton as a future danger or not? In the end, Hilton's fate would be based on a gut feeling.

On Monday, July 22, 1996, day one commenced in the punishment phase of the trial. The prosecutor made an opening statement that, based on the testimony to come, painted a grim picture of Hilton Crawford. Using the metaphor of a theater, he suggested that there was a front-stage Hilton—the family man, father, and coach. This side almost everyone knew and saw. But few people saw or knew the backstage Hilton—a dark manipulator, a person who thought nothing about having a friend murdered when he got caught stealing from his friend.

The defense refrained from making an opening statement.

The prosecutor's first witness was Janice Sapp, a local gemologist. Sapp testified that in 1991, she appraised some jewelry for the Crawfords.

"Why do people want appraisals on their jewelry?"

Sapp told the court that people seek such appraisals for insurance purposes, in case they later need to make a claim on their homeowner's insurance policy if a piece of jewelry is lost or stolen.

The prosecution asked, "Would there be any other reasons why individuals would want appraisals of jewelry?"

Sapp shook her head and replied, "No."

The defense attorney asked Sapp about whether or not her opinions on the worth of gems and stones were subjective. Sapp replied, "Yes."

Ms. Sapp was excused, and Adrian Etheridge, an Allstate insurance agent from Conroe, followed her. He testified that he had known Hilton for fifteen to twenty years as a result of Crawford's being a customer of his. Hilton had homeowner, auto, and life insurance policies with Etheridge.

"Were there any claims ever made by either one of the Crawfords?"

Etheridge said that Hilton filed a claim in January of 1993 for a stolen auto and some personal items contained in the car. The car, he remembered, was worth $20,000, and the missing jewelry, reportedly in the stolen car, was worth $46,000.

"Did Allstate make any payments on the property?"

Etheridge replied, "Yes," and told the court that Allstate paid off the car and made a full payment on the jewelry.

Defense counsel asked the long-time insurance agent if he had any personal knowledge about the missing auto and jewelry.

Etheridge replied, "No."

The defense also asked if he had ever visited the Crawfords in their home.

The witness said that he had and reported that the Crawfords appeared to have a good relationship. Hilton appeared to him to be a good father and a good neighbor. Hilton seemed happy to him. Etheridge, of course, saw only the front-stage Hilton.

The prosecution called Hilton's long-time friend Billy Allen to the stand. Allen, who had testified during the initial phase of the trial, told the court that in 1994, about a year before the crime, Hilton had asked him to store a car in a storage compartment. Allen obliged his friend. The car was drivable but had a window knocked out. Allen said that he stored the car for six or seven months. At some point, Crawford told him that the car had been reported stolen. When Allen learned this, he asked Hilton to remove the vehicle from his property. The stolen vehicle was found by law-enforcement officers when the storage compartments were searched.

Defense counsel asked several more questions about the car and then asked him about Hilton the friend, husband, and father.

"Had he ever," probed the defense attorney, "helped you out when your family was ill or you just needed a friend?"

Allen told the court, "Yes, he visited my family one time when my wife was ill."

"He came to the hospital with you?"

Allen nodded and said, "Yes."

"Do you consider him to be a good friend?"

Allen replied, "Yes, sir, I did."

"Have you seen him with his wife?"

"Yes, sir."

"Have you seen him with his children?"

"Sure," he said.

"Does he seem to be a good husband?"

"Yes, sir," the friend replied.

"Did he seem to be a good father?"

Allen nodded again, "Yes, sir."

Allen went on to say that Hilton was always good to his wife and children, that he cared deeply about his family. The jury continued to hear, at least from Defense Counsel, about the front-stage Hilton.

On cross-examination, the prosecution took aim at the friendship of Hilton and Allen.

"Would a good friend implicate another good friend in the capital murder of a twelve-year-old boy?"

Allen quickly replied, "I definitely would not be involved in that."

"You feel like Mr. Crawford played on your friendship?"

Allen paused. "Yes, sir, I do."

"You feel like Mr. Crawford abused your friendship?"

The damage had been done, and Allen further distanced himself from Crawford "I do that, too." It must have been increasingly difficult for Hilton to sit and watch his friends cast doubts on long-time relationships. It would get even worse.

Sam Petro, who had known Hilton for nearly twenty years, took the stand next. The prosecution asked about how he and Hilton had met one another. Petro said he first got to know Hilton when their kids were involved in Little League. Petro said that he and Hilton played golf together, went on trips together, and attended Superbowl parties together. Petro also said that he and Hilton had been business partners in a restaurant named IZZO'S in Conroe. Once again, the jury was allowed to see the front-stage part of Hilton.

However, the prosecution shifted its tone and asked a series of questions that put the spotlight on the backstage part of Hilton's life. "Did you start a security guard business with Hilton?"

Petro replied that he had and that the business relationship between the two men had been a good decision. Petro, who knew nothing about the private-security business, told the court that he knew Hilton had a law enforcement background.

"What did you bring to the business?"

Petro replied, "Well, it was a unique situation in the financing of the business. I was able to provide the . . . to secure the money for the business, and Mr. Crawford was able to provide the security guard expertise end of the business."

"Did he also have some contacts or some work that he could bring into the business?"

Petro said, "Absolutely, yes, sir. He had some very good accounts he brought into the business, yes, sir."

"Do you remember any of those accounts?"

The long-time friend replied, "Louisiana Pacific. I don't recall the names of all of them because they all had big corporate names like the Entex Building, such like that."

"Did you perform any day-to-day functions in that security guard business?"

Petro stated that his role was very limited, primarily to the financial side of things.

"Who actually performed the everyday running of the business?"

"Well," replied Petro, "that was mainly Mr. Crawford because he had the knowledge of the business. I still did not know what it takes to get a security guard business running." Petro was honest. Hilton, in fact, had run the company and had been responsible for bringing in new clients and accounts.

"Was the business successful?"

The business partner and friend said, "I believe the business, itself, was a successful venture. It was torn down by poor infrastructure in the operation of the business."

"What do you mean by poor infrastructure?"

He said, "We had some theft in the business that eventually tore it down. The best that I can relay is that the business is based on hours and hourly billings, and we had sufficient hourly billings and hourly security work. But my business background is in the produce business, and I've been in that business for thirty-some-odd years. I was not as close to the security business venture as I should have and we had a considerable amount of theft, and, as is the case sometimes, you find out a bit too late."

The prosecutor saw an opening and yanked open the door, "How did you find out about the theft?"

Petro informed the court: "We had a company run an audit on the business, and this company was a prospective buyer of the company. They came back to us and said there was a problem. These guys were pretty sophisticated auditors, and they found that we were paying guards that were not actually on the payroll and making checks to people that did not exist. And in this business, unless you're on top of it every minute, you don't know if you've got two hundred or three hundred guards out there working for you, and you trust someone to run the operation and hope that you're getting two hundred guards working for the two hundred checks you cut. And in our case, we were getting like one hundred and eighty-five guards for two hundred checks."

"How many suspects were there?"

Petro calmly replied that there was one primary suspect. He explained: "The person that was the suspect was doing a lot of handling of our payroll and that's how she had access to this, and we found that she had bought a lot of furniture and was spending a lot of money buying TVs and couches and whatever else you put in a house. We were going to pick up the stuff, but we never went."

The prosecutor let this story go for the moment—it would come up later and would be used to undermine the front-stage Hilton. The story, for now, was a seed planted in the minds of the jurors. The prosecutor finished up with a few questions about Hilton's law-enforcement background.

Defense Counsel brought Petro back to the front-stage Hilton and asked, "What kind of coach was Hilton?"

Petro said, "He was very caring, very loving, and very giving. It was a very impressive thing to see Mr. Crawford and others help coach kids, and the other families always appreciated that."

"Didn't he actually go out of his way to help some of the underprivileged kids that were on his team?"

The long-time friend told the court, "Well, he used to take them out—he'd take them out to pizza. He'd take them out to the park for things. I remember a couple of kids, inner-city kids that he bought bicycles for. Just things of that nature, just very giving, he was a very giving person, always giving things to others."

Petro relayed this information to the jury in a warm and caring manner. He was trying to help his friend. Petro was not lying, nor was he exaggerating as he described how Hilton was good with children and how he helped a number of them from poor backgrounds.

The prosecution came back to shred the sympathy card. "Would it be safe to say he knew how to win the hearts of children?"

To this two-edged dagger of a question, Petro could only answer, "Yes, sir, the children loved him." Petro's answer made Hilton look like an evil pied piper.

The next witness was James Gaffney, a drug dealer, who was doing time in a federal prison in Texas. Gaffney said that he had known Hilton for twelve years and that the two got to know each other in the security business. Gaffney testified that his sister had worked for Hilton and that she had gotten into a little bit of trouble with him.

"What type of trouble was she in?"

Gaffney said his sister had embezzled around $60,000 from the security company. He also said that Hilton did not want his sister to get into any trouble because Gaffney's father owned a building where the security company had a large account. "If the company pressed charges," Gaffney said, "they might lose the account." Hilton, he said, wanted to keep things quiet and did not want any trouble.

The story originally begun by Sam Petro was about to be concluded by Gaffney. The prosecutor asked the convict, "What did Hilton say to you about the situation?"

Gaffney replied, "Well, Mr. Crawford said that he was having trouble with his money partner and that he said it would be better off if we could dispose of his money partner."

"Did he say how he wanted to dispose of the partner?"

Gaffney told the court, "Yeah, well, after talking for a while, he wanted me to kill him, to get rid of him."

"How?"

Gaffney said, "Well, he wanted me to shoot him. It was confusing to me. It was kind of a little bit out of character for him, and everything was hitting me all at once."

The chilling testimony clearly illustrated the manipulative and conniving side of Hilton that most people never saw. The backstage

Hilton was now in the spotlight. Petro, the friend, never knew about the murder plot against him until Gaffney told the court. The testimony also showed the jury that Hilton would kill over money. He would kill a friend if he had to.

"What did you tell Mr. Crawford?"

Gaffney said, "Well, I told him I needed some time to think about it. I was kind of confused. I was thinking he was trying to get something on me because I thought he was taping my conversation, trying to get something on me to go against my father. I told him I had to think about it and I left his office."

"Did you talk with him again about Mr. Crawford wanting you to kill his partner?"

"Yes, I did. He called me on the phone a couple of times. He would start asking me questions and he was going on the assumption, you know, trying to get me to commit that I would do it."

The convict told the court that at one point he met Hilton in the rear of an apartment complex and Hilton gave him a loaded revolver to commit the killing.

"Did Mr. Crawford tell you how he wanted you to shoot his partner?"

Gaffney said that Hilton was going to get Petro to come to the house of his sister, the embezzler, to pick up some furniture.

"Then what?"

Gaffney replied that Hilton would get the partner to roll down his car window and "I was supposed to reach in and shoot him at least twice in the head and then to hurry up and get out of there." Gaffney said sometime later he gave the gun back to Hilton and said that the deal was off.

Defense Counsel attempted to discredit Gaffney's testimony by showing that Gaffney received a sentence reduction as a result of his testimony. But Gaffney, whose sixty-month sentence had been reduced to nineteen months, testified that the reduction was the result of a plea bargain prior to the Crawford case. The defense attorney also asked Gaffney about Hilton the family man and friend. Gaffney reported that he had been to Crawford's home six or seven times to swim and play basketball. He said that he was treated by Hilton as a family member. Gaffney also said that when he was arrested, Crawford sent him money to get out of jail.

Next, Teresa Mobley, a bankruptcy attorney from Houston, testified that the Crawfords filed for bankruptcy in May 1995.

"This is not his [Hilton's] first trip down bankruptcy lane, is it?"

Mobley told the court that Crawford had filed for personal bankruptcy in 1987 when the restaurant IZZO'S closed down. Defense Counsel argued that some of the property listed in the 1995 bankruptcy petition, a race horse called Rather Rapid, was owned partly by Hilton and other associates.

Carl Everett took the stand next, and the prosecutor asked the victim's father about McKay's relationship with Hilton. Carl retold the story about his and McKay's visit to Hilton's house just three weeks prior to the kidnapping. As they were leaving Crawford's house, McKay walked over to Hilton and thanked him for playing basketball with him. Carl repeated that McKay kissed Hilton on the forehead. Everett also told the court that McKay even remembered Hilton in his prayers. This testimony about a tender moment and bedtime prayers underscored the depth of McKay's trust in Hilton Crawford. In McKay's mind, Hilton was indeed an uncle. Through this testimony the prosecution showed how manipulative and dangerous Hilton really was.

The damage had been done, and Defense Counsel could gain nothing by questioning the father. Carl returned to the audience. The State also rested, believing that it had proven beyond a reasonable doubt that Hilton had caused the death of McKay Everett and that Hilton was a continuing threat to society. After all, Hilton had murdered a twelve-year-old boy for the sake of money and even conspired to kill his friend and business partner over money.

The punishment phase resumed on Wednesday, July 24, 1996, and Defense Counsel was prepared to offer testimony that Hilton should be spared from lethal injection. The first witness for the defense was Carrie Alexander, Hilton's aunt. She offered insight about Hilton's front-stage persona—the good son, the obedient son, the dutiful son, and the kindly nephew. She told the jury about the time Hilton took his mother and his own family to Hawaii. She also talked about how Hilton would go over to his parents' house and clean the whole place. The good son did this because his mother was sick with cancer.

The defense attorney asked the aunt, "Is there anything you would like to say to the jury about what you would like to see as the outcome?"

In all honesty, and with genuine human feeling and emotion, she told the court, "Well, I'd like to see him alive."

The prosecution asked Alexander whether children "sort of followed him and looked up to him?" The good aunt replied, "Yes." Hilton again was cast as manipulator.

Next, Aileen Graybill testified she had met Connie Crawford and Paulette Everett at B.B. Rice Elementary School in the early 1980s. She testified that she had known the Crawfords for years and had taken trips with them to Las Vegas and had been to their home several times. She said Hilton was a good husband that he cooked dinners and cleaned up the kitchen.

"How did he treat his wife, Connie?"

She replied, "In my experience, he put her on a pedestal. He kept her in the protective bubble, as far as her never paying the bills or never pumping her own gas in her car."

"Did this incident that Hilton has been convicted of, did that surprise you?"

Aileen, who had only witnessed Hilton's front-stage persona, replied in all honesty, "Yes." To Aileen, the whole series of events was out of character for her nephew. She reiterated her shock by telling the court, "The whole thing is unimaginable to me."

The prosecution asked Ms. Graybill additional questions about Hilton's relationship with his own children.

She reported that Hilton was never verbally abusive and never raised his voice at his children. The answers supported the public Hilton, the Hilton that most people saw.

The defense called to the stand Michael Hoffland, who stated that he had been a family friend for twelve or thirteen years. Hoffland told the court that he had frequently played basketball with the Crawford children at the Crawford house when they were growing up. He stated, again in all honesty, that Hilton was a good man, who had always been there for his family. He said that Hilton idolized his children. Michael stated that Hilton was always outgoing and friendly and never abusive to anyone. He never saw Hilton lose his temper with anyone.

"Do you have a recommendation or opinion you'd like to express to the jury about what should happen today?"

Hoffland asked the jury to spare Hilton's life. The prosecution then asked Hoffland a few brief questions about Crawford's relationship with his children and let the witness go.

Calvin Mathis, who was 28, offered more testimony about the public Hilton, the coach, the decent family man, the funny guy, and the good sport. Mathis told the court that he had played basketball with the Crawford boys when they were kids. Mathis had known Hilton since he was ten years old. Like the other character witnesses, Mathis told the jury that Hilton was a proud family man and that he was kind to other people. Mathis said that Hilton had treated him like a son.

Mathis also asked the jury to spare Crawford's life. In an emotional statement he said, "I just think that you know, he should do his time in prison and that's going to kill him more than anything. Right now, I just don't understand this. I mean, the man—he's not, he's not, I mean the man sitting there is not the man I know."

The prosecution countered this "good feeling" testimony by asking Mathis, "The man you know is not the man in your mind that created this crime, is it?" Mathis agreed. Finally, the prosecution asked Mathis, "Would you agree with me that Mr. Crawford has two faces?"

Mathis struggled with the question and told the jury he only knew the man in front of him, the man he saw. He said he never saw a second side.

Rick Pearce, now 27, another boyhood pal of Hilton's sons, offered more testimony about how nice Hilton was to his sons and wife. As a youngster he frequently spent the night at the Crawfords. He played basketball with Kevin and Hilton. He said Hilton adored his two sons and never lost his temper. Pearce said that as a coach Hilton made sure everyone played. Pearce even attended professional basketball and baseball games with the Crawfords. In fact, the Pearces and Crawfords took vacations together. There was no doubt that Hilton was a good husband and father. No testimony was offered to counter the image of Hilton the family man. Children trusted him, he said. The defense attorney asked, "Were you surprised when Hilton Crawford was arrested for this crime?"

Pearce nodded and replied, "I was shocked. I never imagined

that would have happened. To this day I am still shocked by what happened."

Pearce asked the jury to spare Hilton's life. The prosecution asked if Pearce trusted Hilton, and he said that he did. Further testimony revealed that Pearce would have gone anywhere with Hilton, had Hilton asked him.

Susan Crawford, age 29, the wife of Crawford's son Chris, testified next. She told the court that she had known Hilton for eleven years. The witnesses were now getting closer to Crawford in an attempt to show everyone the good Hilton. The defense attorney was using the inner circle to save his life.

"Over the last eleven years, prior to, except last year, how often were you around Hilton Crawford?"

"At least once a week" said Susan.

"Were you in his home?"

"Yes, sir."

"Did he visit you in your and Chris's home?"

"Yes," replied Susan.

The defense attorney continued, "So you've seen him basically on hundreds of occasions?"

"Yes, sir."

"During the eleven-year period and hundreds of times you've been around the defendant, have you ever seen him lose his temper?"

Susan replied, "No, never." She went on to tell the jury that Hilton had never acted abusively toward her, Connie Crawford, or the Crawford boys. She said that Hilton was involved in the YMCA and had been active in the Make a Wish Foundation.

"How would you describe the relationship to this jury that you saw over that eleven-year period?"

Susan replied, "Just that he was a very good family man. He always took care of his family."

"Did he look after Connie in some sort of special way?"

Susan told the court, "He bought her clothes. He bought her cars and picked out her furniture, her appliances. She didn't even know how to pump gas—I had to show her how to do that."

"What are your feelings toward the defendant?"

Susan said, "I love him." It was an emotional moment.

"Is the crime that the defendant has been convicted of, is this totally out of character for the Hilton Crawford that you knew for eleven years and were around on hundreds of occasions?"

Susan said, "Yes, sir, it is, and I want the jury to spare his life."

But the prosecutor chipped away at her testimony by bringing up the front-stage and backstage Hilton.

"So it turns out you really didn't know a side of Hilton Crawford at all, did you?"

Susan agreed with the prosecutor in that she saw or knew only the good, kind, caring side of Hilton, and that Hilton hid from her his ability to beat and shoot a child to death, to leave a child behind in a swamp. Despite the other side of Hilton, she still asked the jury to show mercy and spare his life.

More of the good side of Hilton was paraded before the jury when Christopher Crawford, Hilton's elder son, took the stand. It was a difficult moment, an emotional moment, and a tragic moment all at the same time because here was a son desperately trying to save his father. This was not how things worked—normally fathers try to help and save their children. Not here. Now it was time for the son to plead for mercy, to plead for his father's life. As expected, Chris told the jury that his father was not a violent person.

"One time," he said, "I took the car when I was fourteen and kind of wrecked it. He got a little upset then, but he had very good reason to. He didn't beat me or anything for any reason."

Chris repeated what the other witnesses had said about Hilton the coach, how Hilton had always been involved in youth sports, how he had coached little boys and opened his house for teammates and the neighborhood kids. Though the jury had heard it all before, Chris's testimony was particularly genuine and heartfelt, and seemed even more real than that of any of his predecessors.

The defense attorney asked Chris, "What kind of relationship did your dad and mom have?"

The son replied, "They had a very normal, loving relationship. We never had no problems. I never seen any kind of violence. He always respected her. He basically treated her like a queen all the time. He gave her everything."

"Have you seen a change in your mother since your dad has been arrested and in jail?"

Chris had only one answer: "Very much so. You know, she's . . . I mean her whole world basically collapsed on her. She's been at the point of a nervous breakdown for a long time, and she doesn't think clearly. She's definitely been affected by it." He also told the jury that Connie's house had been shot at three times.

The defense attorney asked Chris, "Based on everything you know about your father over all of the years, is this action your father has been convicted of totally, completely out of character with the man you have known since your birth?"

"Yes, it is."

On cross-examination, the prosecutor asked, "Did your father gamble?"

Chris replied, "Yes he did. The race horses—he'd do a little gambling at the racehorse tracks. He'd bet a little on football games. Besides that, you know, it wasn't nothing major, wasn't like a big thing going on or anything."

"What do you mean, a big thing?"

"Well, I just meant, he'd gamble some on just sports games and stuff. It didn't seem like he was gambling all the time, is what I'm trying to say. I mean, I never noticed he had a problem like that. I never noticed a problem that would have affected our family."

The prosecutor, in more questioning, brought up the idea of the two-sided Hilton.

"Would you agree with me there's a side to your father that no one, even you, could ever have dreamed would come out?"

The son replied, "Yes, sir." It was true. The son, who was trying to save his father, had never seen the other side. He even said that their family had a good relationship with the Everetts.

Kevin Crawford, the second and youngest son, followed his brother, and his testimony matched that of the previous witnesses. Kevin had attended the University of Houston and served with the men's basketball team as a team manager.

The defense asked, "Were there occasions when basketball players from foreign countries would come in and stay at your house, your family's house?"

Kevin said, "Yeah, all the time, all types of players would stay at our house. The players loved him. My first college roommate called him *Mr. American Father*."

Kevin went on and told the court about the front-stage Hilton. He told the jury that his father had been a baseball coach, a good husband, and a good father. He said that his father had paid for a limousine and dinner on his prom night. He testified that he had never seen his father lose his temper or act violently towards other people. Kevin said that his father had protected their family from his financial problems. He said that he loved his father in spite of the crime and asked the jury to spare his father's life.

On cross-examination, the prosecutor asked Kevin about his use of credit cards. Kevin offered that he procured, legally, an American Express card and later a Visa card. He told the jury that Hilton cosigned on the American Express card. Kevin told the court that altogether he had thirteen credit cards in his name, but that only two were in his possession.

The prosecutor asked, "Who kept the other cards?"

Kevin responded, "My father kept them at his home."

"Now was there a time that you became aware that you had some pretty hefty bills on some credit cards?"

Kevin said, "Well, in mid-September 1995, the police released the contents of my father's briefcase and stuff with my name on it, and that's when I became aware of that."

The prosecutor asked, "Tell the jury how much total had been run up without your knowledge, fraudulently, by your father on your credit cards that you didn't know about."

Kevin had to tell the truth: "$75,000." The son told the court that he examined the invoices and saw that his father had used the cards to purchase home amenities, restaurant meals, and even cash advances in the amounts of $1,500, $750, and $800. The spending spree took place between June of 1995 and September of 1995. Hilton had spent $75,000 in the four months preceding the kidnapping and murder of McKay Everett.

The prosecutor went on: "Before September 12, 1995, you trusted your father, didn't you?"

Kevin replied, "Yes, sir."

"You could never in your wildest imagination believe that your father would be the prime party, the actual person, the actual person that did a murder-for-hire plot?"

Kevin said, "No, no, sir."

"You trusted your father, didn't you?"

"Yes, sir," said the heartbroken son.

"He violated that trust, didn't he?"

Kevin said, "Yes, sir."

"Did you have anything to do with McKay?"

Kevin told the court, "I babysat him occasionally, stuff like he would be at the house, or like when he came over, I'd show him about computers."

"Did he seem to you to be a pretty smart little boy?"

"Yes, he was. He was real smart."

"Do you think McKay trusted your father?"

"Yes, sir," said Kevin.

"Your daddy violated that trust, didn't he?"

The question, in all its simplicity, hit the courtroom like a ton of bricks. The room became quiet. The fateful question also summarized the entire trial and totally revealed the essence of Hilton Crawford.

Kevin bravely said, "Yes, sir."

The defense attorney then had a chance for additional questions. "Kevin, in spite of all of this, do you still love your father?" The defense tried to reset the jury's mind about the good Hilton.

The shell-shocked son nodded and said, "Yes, very much."

"Are you still asking the jury to spare his life?"

Kevin looked at the jury and replied, "Yes, yes."

Kevin Crawford's testimony ended the morning session of the punishment phase. A break was in order after the morning's emotional testimony. The defense was set to call one more—one last—witness to argue that Hilton's life should be spared. The trial of the century was nearing its end. Only a few more questions were left. By now, everyone was nearly exhausted, and the long ordeal for both Paulette and Hilton was just about over. Had the jury made up its mind? Would any more testimony affect the outcome?

It was now 1 p.m. and the audience was seated, waiting for the finale. The jurors were led in and they took their seats in unison. In came the judge; on cue, everyone rose and then sat down on orders from the bailiff. It came to one last ritual for one last witness.

"Call your next witness," said the Judge.

"The defense would call Dr. Walter Quijano."

When Quijano was sworn in, the defense asked, "Would you tell the jury some of your educational background, about your professional background, that qualifies you for the position and the work you do now?"

Quijano said, "I have a bachelor's degree in general psychology, a master's degree in clinical psychology, and a doctorate degree also in clinical psychology. My experiences have been in both the private and public sectors. I have been staff psychologist at the Federal Correctional Institute at Terminal Island in San Pedro, California, and been staff psychologist in the Texas Department of Corrections doing chemical-dependency work. I served as Director of Psychiatric Services and Chief Psychologist for the Texas Department of Corrections from 1983 to 1988. I opened a private practice in Conroe. I do evaluations and treatment of activities for the local probation department and district courts. I also have my normal clinical cases on a day-to-day basis, referred to me by various sources."

"What do you do when you make a consultation in a criminal case?"

The doctor told the court, "Generally, depending on the questions, I would do a psychological evaluation, a competency-to-stand-trial evaluation, and an insanity evaluation. In capital cases, future-dangerousness evaluations and in some instances, just assisting the judge in determining conditions of bond for people who have gone to, or want to get out of, jail."

"How many capital cases have you been involved in making evaluations on, Dr. Quijano?'

"I have been involved in more than seventy capital cases."

Dr. Quijano was no ordinary suburban psychologist with a caseload of ornery kids or soccer moms who had lost their men to younger women. Quijano, chief psychologist for the Texas prison system from 1983-1988, had been around criminals and knew their traits. More importantly, he was a veteran of the Texas death circuit. He knew the routine. He knew the questions beforehand. His specialty was evaluating the future dangerousness of criminals like Hilton Crawford. He was also a switch hitter, as he had worked on behalf of both the defense and prosecution. He commanded respect, and the jury listened attentively.

The defense counsel asked, "On how many separate occasions did you see Mr. Crawford?"

Quijano told the court that he had met with Hilton three times, for about a total of six hours. Quijano said that he gave Hilton a personality test and an achievement test. The defendant came out with an IQ of 94, which, the expert said, was in the "normal range." He also said that Hilton did not suffer from any mental defect or disease. Quijano said that Hilton was competent and that he understood the difference between right and wrong. According to Quijano, Crawford appreciated the seriousness of the offense and the punishment associated with the offense. He understood the proceedings against him and had assisted in his own defense. Hilton, testified Quijano, was sane.

The idea that Hilton was sane resonated well in the minds of the audience and the jury. Everyone in the courtroom had watched Hilton over the last month, and he had appeared normal. He had dressed in coat and tie, and as he sat there he had appeared to listen to the testimony. He never lashed out or acted in any visibly odd manner that might have led the jury to think that he was incompetent.

The only remaining issue was whether or not Hilton was dangerous.

The defense asked, "Did you do further tests and evaluations to determine the future dangerousness of the defendant?"

"Yes," said Dr. Quijano.

The defense asked, "Did you form an opinion as to the probability issue, that the defendant would commit criminal acts of violence that would constitute a continuing threat to society?"

The psychologist said, "Yes," and proceeded to tell the jury the basis of his professional evaluation.

Quijano explained, "The basis of my opinions are the details of the crime, the person's history, the person's background and the place where he will be. These were used to consider the degree of dangerousness in the future."

"Would you explain in detail each of these categories, please?"

Quijano agreed. To this point in the trial, members of the jury had heard and were asked to consider a wide variety of evidence. They had seen hard evidence about ballistics, forensics, insects, blood spatters, bullet cartridges, phone records, and DNA and fingerprints.

Quijano's evidence was something different for the jury. It was gray, subjective, and difficult to see, touch, or grasp. No matter, the jury listened intently.

The expert witness explained: "The first category contains the details of this crime itself. In this category, we find that this defendant has no chronic or repeated history of assault or violence, so we had to look at what could have pushed him to commit this crime. What we have found was there were a long series of financial manipulations and financial schemes that finally drove him into a point of desperation and he did this very serious and heinous act. The second factor is his personality style and his history. Again there is no evidence of assaultiveness, violence. This is not a person with a violent and assaultive lifestyle. This offense was peculiar and atypical of him. There are histories of other financial foolishness, but not assaultiveness. Given that fifty-seven years of no documented history of violence or assaultiveness. He was not chronically violent.

"The next factor is the pressure that must have pushed this typically nonviolent person into committing a very, very violent act. What is the pressure, and is the pressure still present or is it gone? If it is gone, then the degree of dangerousness will, of course, be dropped. And finally, where do you expect this person to be in the future, where his dangerousness is being predicted? We predict, of course, that he'll be in the prison, and in that setting, the probability of committing another violent act would approach the lower end of the spectrum."

"So, what is your testimony as to your prediction of future violence of the defendant?" Here it was the question that finally mattered in Hilton Crawford vs. The State of Texas.

Quijano, the expert of the mind, the professional reader of behavior in the here and now and predictor of behavior in the future said, "My testimony is that in a continuum of very little dangerousness to very extreme dangerousness, he would be placed in the lower end of the spectrum, given the conditions that I have set."

The psychologist had made some points with the jury. Research suggests that the earlier a person engages in criminal activity, the more likely it is that the person will continue to commit crime. The best predictor of future behavior is past behavior. Hilton had no documented violent criminal acts in his past with which to connect a straight line that would point to future violence. In terms of official misconduct, Hilton had a clean slate. He lacked a police record, he was not a criminal—a killer, yes, but he was no career criminal.

The prosecution asked Quijano about life in prison, the classification of prisoners, and how Hilton might fare in prison should he be given a life sentence. Quijano told the jury that if Hilton, the ex-cop, went to prison, he would more likely be a victim than a predator. Ex-cops have a hard time in the joint. So do child killers. But if dangerousness could be measured by a thermometer, Hilton had a very low temperature.

The prosecutor added, "If he gets death, that danger would go down, too, won't it?"

The expert agreed and said, "Definitely."

In the end, all the psychologist could offer was a subjective opinion about Hilton Crawford's future. His opinion was, in fact, an emotional plea by a doctor, like those offered by friends and relatives, to spare Crawford's life. But the funny thing about future dangerousness is that no one really knows a person's future. Violence, or any kind of human behavior for that matter, cannot accurately be predicted. A psychologist can never say for certain that a person will never be violent again. Juries pick up on this uncertainty and are primed to vote for execution. Death cures all ambiguity.

The prosecution called one last witness, who commented on prisoner classification and life on death row. The testimony of this witness, though interesting to ordinary people as it delved into prison life, mattered little in the jurors' minds. Once this witness was excused, the defense rested. It was over. The Trial of the Century had ended, and now the fate of Hilton Crawford rested in the hands of the twelve people selected to listen to all of the evidence.

Jury deliberations began around 5:00 p.m., and at 7:00 p.m. the jury told the court that they had arrived at a verdict. The jury agreed that Hilton was a future threat, that he had in fact, caused the death of McKay Everett and that there was no evidence to warrant a life sentence. In everyday language, they recommended that Hilton Crawford get the needle. The verdict, though dramatic, was expected.

The most dramatic moment in the trial was now at hand. Texas law provides that a victim or close relative of the victim can address the court at the conclusion of formal sentencing.

Paulette read a prepared statement. Once again she came face to face with Crawford. Several weeks ago she was the sobbing, hysterical mother who had to be taken out of the courtroom. Now she faced Hilton with a calm confidence that struck nearly everyone in the room. She spoke about her enormous loss and how, as with any mother, her son had been the light of her life. She made McKay live in the minds of the audience, reminding them that this twelve-year-old boy had touched many people. Throughout her statement, Hilton hung his head and refused to look at Paulette.

She said, "I do not have an answer to Hilton's actions. I cannot speak for Hilton. I try to imagine what McKay would say to Hilton if he were here to speak. Words fail me. Silence speaks at my house. I hope McKay's last words will forever sound in Hilton's ears. I know McKay angered Hilton by his words. I know my son fought for his life." Paulette made a few concluding comments about her struggle to live. And then it was over. This was the most powerful scene in the trial.

Hilton was whisked off to death row to start a different life. Paulette and Carl drove home to an empty house to start a different life. Hilton's and Paulette's roads drifted apart, once again, only to intersect in one final piece of drama. In the meantime, Paulette would fight to restore her life, to remain alive in a world that could only be described as hellish. The same could be said for Hilton.

Chapter 9

Beacons in the Trees

I have always wondered about how Hilton pulled this off. During the trial, I sat there and watched him and tried to figure out when he started his plan. There is no way he just dreamed this up one day and did it, took McKay away. He had a plan—I know he had a plan. I'll go to my grave believing he had a plan. I've lost a lot of sleep over thinking about signs. I mean, there had to be signs of his planning. I just missed the whole thing. If I had seen his signs, maybe I could have prevented the whole thing. This part just kills me, you know. Maybe there was something I should have seen and taken action on. Hilton committed an incredibly stupid crime, but he was no dummy. He planned the kidnapping—at what point, though, I don't know. I don't know when the planning began, but he had a plan. It wasn't a spur-of-the-moment thing—he planned it. On the outside he was nice to McKay, but on the inside he was planning to kidnap my son. He had a plan.

Criminal trials are miniature plays, complete with a series of acts, actors, lines, plots, and subplots. In the final act, the jury must sort through the lines delivered by the actors and craft a review or make a decision. In Hilton Crawford's trial the evidence was laid out and he was found guilty. But what really happened? In this chapter we lay out the pieces of the puzzle to offer another perspective on the events of September 12, 1995. The key to our understanding of the crime lies in the evolution of a piece of modern technology, the cell phone. The cell phone helped put Crawford on death row.

The mid-nineteenth century was an era of tremendous scientific experimentation in a wide variety of areas, and the extraordinary

English chemist Michael Faraday made new discoveries in the nature of electricity. In the 1840s, he conducted numerous experiments on whether or nor space could conduct electricity. His views were disputed by the great minds of the day, but his work spurred on others. A Virginia dentist took Faraday's ideas, and in the 1860s and 1870s transmitted telegraph messages between two mountains that lay nearly twenty miles apart. He used the earth's atmosphere and kites as conductors.

Once an idea comes out of a box, it takes little time before new applications are developed. Early attempts at wireless communication were refined and further refined over the years. In the 1940s, the first mobile wireless phone systems were seen in the United States. The service and technology associated with this form of communication were very expensive and use was very limited. It was not until the 1970s that the first portable handsets were available and people could communicate between mobile phones. The first public cell phones were introduced in 1977. The advent of cell phones has had a significant impact on human communication. Today they are a necessary ingredient in ordinary life and are now part of our culture.

Cell phones, no matter how small or how thin, operate like a radio. The phone picks up signals from towers within its cellular system. Each tower or base station covers a circular area called a cell. Large metropolitan areas usually have hundreds of these towers to allow large numbers of customers convenient use.

All cell phones have special codes that are needed to identify the owner, phone, and the service provider used by the owner. The code functions basically like a social security number or driver's license and assists in customer identification. The code facilitates billing. No matter where the customer calls from, or at what time, a usage log is created.

The other interesting aspect of cell phones concerns the towers. A person placing a call while moving in a car is transferred from one base station to the next. As a result of this technology a car-bound caller can maintain a conversation from one city to the next, from one county to the next, and even from one state to the next. These "hand-offs" are also logged. While cell phones have certainly made personal communication easier, they have also undermined personal privacy.

Usage is logged, making a person's whereabouts easily known. When used, they function like hand-held homing devices.

There were several witnesses employed by a cellular phone service that testified about calls made from Hilton's cell phone between September 11, 1995, and September 15, 1995. Hilton's calls provided a log of his whereabouts, but these logs represent only one piece of the crime puzzle. In this chapter, we attempted to reconstruct the events of September 12, 1995. However, the events of that fateful night were set in motion months before.

We believe that Hilton hatched his plan to kidnap McKay Everett around the time he filed for bankruptcy. This was in May of 1995. We also believe that the impending bankruptcy drove Hilton to plan the unthinkable: the murder of a child. His "unshareable problem" became so burdensome that murder became his means to an end. The pressures to pay up, to live the good life, to be somebody, to be respectable, converged on Hilton at the same time, and murder, no matter how twisted the thought, was the way out.

The first evidence of Hilton's plans for kidnapping McKay came from a voluntary written statement made by Billy Joe Cox to the police on January 8, 1996. Cox, a security guard who worked for Hilton, clued in law enforcement officials to an interesting conversation he had with Hilton around August 15, 1995.

Cox wrote in his statement:

> On or about August 15 [1995], I had a conversation with Hilton Crawford in regards to how long it would take a dead body to begin to put off an odor. My remark was that rigor mortis enters the body within twenty-four hours and leaves the body within forty-eight hours. Hilton asked, "How long before a body would put off an odor inside a trunk of a car." I said it depends on the weather. Hilton said, "What if it is hot weather and inside a trunk of a car." I told him three to four days. He was aware that I had been in the funeral business for twenty-two years.

This conversation between Cox and Crawford occurred approximately one month before McKay's abduction. The content of the conversation clearly suggested that Hilton was making plans to kidnap McKay.

One of the most nagging issues for victims or survivors centers on why they did not see the tragedy coming. Were there any signs to tip off the crime? When, right after the kidnapping, the FBI questioned Carl and Paulette about their relationship with Hilton, they asked if Hilton had ever wanted to take McKay out alone to play or go get ice cream. The Everetts told the FBI that in August of 1995 Hilton had indeed asked the Everetts if he could possibly pick up McKay after school and take him for yogurt. He also wanted to come by the house to pick up McKay to get pizza. Hilton also asked the Everetts if he and McKay could go to the park one afternoon to play.

According to Paulette, these requests were turned down. It never dawned on them, however, that Hilton was planning an abduction. The FBI told the Everetts that predators usually have backup plans when their original tactics fail. Hilton was also seeking times when McKay might be alone.

Sometime in mid-August of 1995, J. Herrin, a friend of Hilton's from his horse track days, testified that Hilton offered him $80,000 to "baby-sit" a kid for a few days. Hilton told Herrin not to worry because the kid would be returned, unhurt, to the parents. Herrin testified that he declined Hilton's offer.

In late August, Carl and McKay visited Hilton at his home in Conroe. McKay and Hilton played basketball and threw a football around. McKay even kissed "Uncle Hilty" on his forehead as they were departing. Hilton presented his cover as the "good uncle," all the while making plans to abduct McKay. Indeed, the basketball outing was an opportune time to keep McKay at ease and comfortable around Hilton.

Another important piece of information underscoring Hilton's abduction plans came from Joe Duhon, the trainer of Crawford's race horses in Louisiana, to whom he owed training fees. Duhon made a written statement on October 14, 1995, about a conversation he had with Hilton in the early part of September 1995. Duhon also testified about the conversation during the trial.

Duhon wrote:

During the early days of September 1995 he [Hilton] had something going on real big and he was going to pay for everything. He was selling some timber and he would pay me off. We talked on the phone, strictly business. He made a statement on the phone, just casual conversation of if he didn't get the money he would kill himself or somebody. I didn't care what he did, I wanted my money, and it was strictly business.

It was now around September 5, 1995, and Hilton had decided to kidnap McKay. He needed the ransom money to pay off his debts and to purchase a new home in a flashy golf community on Lake Conroe. All he lacked was a way to get to McKay while the boy was alone. McKay had to be alone. It must have dawned on Hilton at this time that the upcoming Amway meeting, scheduled for 8:00 p.m. on September 12, was the perfect opportunity to take McKay. He had to make sure the Everetts were attending.

Irene Flores, in her written statement and trial testimony, stated that Hilton contacted her around September 8, 1995, and asked her if she wanted "to make some money." Crawford wanted Flores to make one phone call, and she would make $30,000. Crawford also told Flores that the Everetts were divorced and that Paulette wanted to take McKay and run away with the ransom money.

September 12, 1995, arrived and Hilton was preparing to kidnap McKay. His cover was a scheduled business trip to check on employees and security arrangements at the company's East Texas plants. Around 5 p.m. Hilton called the Everett residence to verify that Carl and Paulette were going to the Amway meeting. Again Paulette assured Hilton that she and Carl were going to the meeting. Once Hilton received this information, he waited. Paulette and Randy Bartlett departed around 8 p.m.

Hilton and Connie Crawford went to Connie's sister's house for dinner around 5 p.m. The Crawfords ate a fast supper because Connie had to get to choir practice and Hilton told them that he had to take care of some security arrangements at a nearby business in New Waverly. The couple headed home around 6:30 p.m. Sometime around 7 p.m. Hilton left his residence and filled the gas tank in the gold LHS.

Around 8:25 p.m., he drove up the back driveway of the Everett residence and went to the rear entrance. Hilton was family, and he was welcome at the back door. At the same time Hilton was knocking on the door, McKay was on the phone with Elizabeth Schaeffer. She testified that McKay called her at 8:30 p.m. but a minute later McKay told her to "hold on," in reference to the knock at the back door. McKay never resumed the conversation, and Elizabeth took another phone call from a friend.

Hilton knocked on the door and McKay probably peeked through the curtain to see who was there. It was Hilton Crawford, Uncle Hilty. Seeing Hilton at the back door probably eased McKay's thoughts. Then Hilton told McKay that Carl and Paulette had been injured in a car accident on the way to the Amway meting. Hilton asked McKay to come with him to the hospital.

McKay trusted Hilton. He dutifully shut off the home security system, hung up the telephone, and hurriedly left with Hilton. The back door was left ajar. After all, it was a medical emergency and McKay was no doubt frightened. The boy ran out the back door without his shoes on. Hilton got in the car behind the steering wheel and McKay jumped into the front passenger seat. The gold car quickly backed down the driveway and nearly hit Bill Kahn's garbage cans. The car sped away around 8:35 p.m. It was already dark because the sun, as the season was moving into fall, had set at 7:37 p.m.

Hilton had a mobile phone, and at 8:37 p.m. he called Irene Flores. The call lasted two minutes and twenty-nine seconds. He told Irene that he had McKay and to use the pay phone to call Carl later that evening and to follow through with the ransom demand and instructions.

McKay was an intelligent young man, and when he heard this phone conversation, he must have known that something was very wrong. He was alarmed and probably asked Hilton a number of questions about what was going on and what really happened to his parents.

We believe that Hilton, riled by these questions, pulled off the road somewhere just outside the Everetts' subdivision, used the push button to open the trunk, and yanked McKay out of the car. Once outside the car, Hilton hit McKay with a hard blow to the left side of his face. The blow broke several bones in the boy's facial area. It also stunned McKay and probably knocked him out. Hilton threw McKay in the trunk and quickly sped off.

He exited the subdivision, took Loop 336 to Interstate 45, and drove south about one mile and exited on Highway 105. He continued to place a number of calls that evening. The beacons in the trees logged his travel on the way to Whiskey Bay.

The distance between Conroe and Beaumont, near the state line, is roughly a hundred miles, and Highway 105 is a two-lane highway that cuts through the Piney Woods of East Texas. Travel time is roughly ninety minutes. While in Conroe, he called his home at 8:53 p.m., a call that lasted forty seconds. From the Cleveland area he called his home again at 9:10 p.m. This second call lasted thirty-three seconds. We do not know if he talked to anyone or simply left a message.

At 10:15 p.m. Hilton placed another call home from Beaumont. The call lasted sixty seconds. The gold LHS, with its child cargo, found its way to Interstate 10 and sped towards the Louisiana border.

Hilton called home again at 11:09 p.m., this time from Lake Charles, Louisiana. The call lasted sixty seconds. At 11:10 p.m. he made a two-minute call from Lake Charles to Irene Flores. She told Hilton that she had not yet spoken to Carl Everett. He called Flores again at 11:13 p.m. They talked for three minutes, and Hilton told her to keep trying to reach Carl. Hilton waited seventeen more minutes until he called Flores again. He must have been frantic. He talked to Flores at 11:30 p.m. The call, again from Lake Charles, lasted six minutes. Flores told Hilton that, finally, after thirty to fifty attempts, she had reached Carl and given him the instructions.

With this information in hand, Hilton proceeded to Whiskey Bay. The approximate distance from Lake Charles to Lafayette is seventy-six miles and another thirty to the swamp. It took Hilton about ninety minutes to reach the swamp. However, along the way the pounding and yelling from the trunk by McKay escalated and increased by the mile. Somewhere between Lake Charles and Lafayette, Hilton pulled over, opened the trunk, and bludgeoned McKay senseless. McKay was struck with a hard blow to the right side of his skull, perhaps with a metal flashlight or a handgun. His skull was crushed, and he was rendered unconscious. Hilton got back inside the car and proceeded east. The blow to McKay's head also spattered blood in the rear of the trunk.

Crawford pulled off I-10 at the Whiskey Bay exit onto the

shell road off Louisiana Road 975. He dragged the unconscious boy through the weeds along a fence past a utility pole. The boy's body was tossed in the weeds about eight feet from a fence post. To make sure the boy was dead, Hilton shot him twice with his .45 handgun.

It was now approximately 2 a.m. and Hilton climbed back in his gold LHS and sped west on I-10. He checked into a Best Western in Beaumont sometime after 4:30 a.m.. Ms. Bambi Carter, night auditor at the hotel, testified that she remembered Crawford as the man who checked in early in the morning of September 13, 1995. She also testified that Crawford's appearance was normal, and nothing about him seemed unusual.

On the 13th Hilton rose early, called Billy Allen, and drove to Buena, Texas, where he met Allen at his storage shed business. Allen testified that Hilton arrived around 9:00 a.m. and Gary Capo was there too. Capo later testified that Hilton "was not his normal self." Hilton tore the lining out of the trunk and asked Allen to store some articles for him, including the .45 handgun. He gave Allen a bottle of champagne and left, probably around 9:30 a.m. Hilton returned home and went next door to the Schaeffer's at 11 a.m., where he received news of McKay's disappearance. He remained calm and proceeded to make a number of calls to solidify his alibi. He failed in this part of his plan and was arrested at his home on the morning of Friday, September 15, 1995.

In the field of criminal justice it is a fact that witnesses often lie, or make false reports, or fail to remember key facts, or fail to show up for trial. Cell phone towers are just the opposite. These instruments are the perfect silent witness. They don't talk back, they don't fail to remember, and they never misspell a name or a date in a report. The beacons in the trees never lie, as Hilton found out only too late.

We think this is what happened. However, only McKay and Hilton will ever truly know what happened on September 12, 1995. No matter, Crawford was sent packing to death row, and Paulette was forced to rejoin the world.

Chapter 10

Out of the Ashes

It is hard to believe that one day in the life of anybody can totally change it. I am here to tell you that September 12, 1995, changed my life forever. My soul was stomped and spat on. Neither the passage of time, a guilty verdict, therapy, the death penalty, nor seeing Hilton die would reverse the loss of McKay. I cannot say which was destroyed first—my mind, my body, or my spirit—but September 12 destroyed all three. The impact was sudden, and it came out of nowhere. On that day, I felt like I was run over by an eighteen-wheeler. My mind played games with me and rushed forward with denial. My body believed my mind and began to deteriorate. My spirit, my inner songbird, deflated like a popped balloon. The worst part of all of this was that I did not see it coming. How could I? I did not know what to look for. Who does? Hilton gave McKay gifts and played with him. I never saw it coming. Now I have to live without my son. I have no choice but to accept McKay's death.

The trial was finally over and Hilton was to pay for the Crime of the Century with his life. Paulette read her statement to the world. She read it with an air of confidence and strength she had not experienced for years. It was over.

Carl and Paulette thanked their friends for their support and then exited the courtroom. The couple got in their car, physically and mentally exhausted from the ordeal. It had finally sunk in. These two kids from Mississippi, though older than when they came to Texas, were driving home to start a new life, again. The car slowly made its way home. The couple said nothing. What was left to say?

Paulette's mind drifted back to September 12, 1995, as the car turned onto the busy highway. The void left by her completed mission would soon be filled with memories and images of that horrible day. That's how it is with victims—their minds always go back to the day their world stopped. They replay the day's events right up to the tragic moment. Paulette asked herself, "Was there anything I could have done to prevent this?" Torturing herself with guilt, she asked, "Why didn't I see this coming?" She replayed September 12, 1995, again and again. It was maddening. She thought about the exact second, minute, and hour that she was told McKay was missing. Worse, her mind flashed hundreds and thousands of images from the evening of September 12. There were many images of the house on the corner lot with the trees, with the beautiful lawn, with the abundant bushes, and the ever-present yellow crime-scene tape. The yellow tape was everywhere.

The movie in her mind replayed the whole scene frame by agonizing frame. She remembered crouching on the floorboard of her own car, screaming like a wounded animal. When Carl sped up and passed a car, Paulette looked at the floorboard and heard those screams again. It was torture—the screams would never be erased from her memory. Her throat ached from the thought of those awful frightening screams.

Carl asked her, "Why are you so quiet? What are you thinking about?"

Paulette answered, "Oh, nothing, just thinking about everything." Her mind drifted back to September 12. She remembered that the Crawfords had called to check on her and Carl and asked if anyone had heard from McKay. The thought was like a slap across the face. She remembered that neither Hilton nor Connie had ever come to their house during that week from hell, to visit or offer any help. They never showed up at the back door, as so many other friends did.

The car motored down the highway. Paulette remembered how her body had begun to shut down as soon as she heard that McKay was missing. She remembered how her speech had slowed and how difficult it was to form words. It was like she was returning to the days when she was three years old. Her brain, like a cheap transistor radio, had short-circuited. The movie in her mind showed the scene where her arm pulled up. At the same time her speech had slowed.

She could see that her arm bent inwards at the elbow and that she had no control over her it. It was horrifying.

The mental movie showed a friend coming over to her and trying to straighten out her arm. The arm refused to move. The friend's expression was one of fear. The car hit a bump and Carl apologized. The bump brought Paulette back into reality. She laughed to herself and realized that many friends are friends only when the body is whole and presentable. She wondered about people in wheelchairs and how many of them still had the same number of friends after their bodies had been put in metal chairs. Paulette drifted back to September 12 and remembered that her right leg had refused to move. She had been forced to drag it on the floor.

Paulette remembered the FBI and the District Attorney's office telling her and Carl when to talk and what to say. She only wanted to know who had McKay, and she wanted to kill the person who took her son. Dark thoughts surfaced. She wondered if McKay had food and water and whether or not he was allowed to go to the bathroom. Did he suffer? Did he fight Hilton? Was there a struggle? Did he die quickly? It was agonizing to have these thoughts, but her mind raced on. The idea of not knowing what had happened to McKay was absolute torture. This was the worst part of the whole ordeal.

The car pulled off the highway and slowly headed home, through the woods, up the driveway, and into the garage. Carl and Paulette entered the house and commented on how quiet the place seemed. God, it was quiet. And then it really dawned on them—life was now different.

The trial, though important because it made Hilton confront his own demons, did not bring closure to Paulette. Nothing could ever bring closure to the loss of a child. Closure was some clinical word used by others, non-victims, to tell victims to "get over it." Thoughts of McKay were continuous. Paulette was like the victim of an amputation who sensed pain in a lost limb. McKay was gone in the physical sense, but he was everywhere in spirit and in the possessions that were still in the home.

Some victims of violent crimes, like cancer patients, can manage their own levels of pain. Indeed, some individuals have extraordinary thresholds for pain. But Paulette feared for her sanity. She had to do something, *anything*, to regain her life.

To help her with the mental pain, she tried therapy with a local therapist who ran a state-funded facility for recovering alcoholics. She attended therapy sessions and looked around at the men living in the facility. She had as many unseen demons as they did. But she was no alcoholic—she was not addicted to some physical substance. Perhaps she was addicted to grief, an unseen substance that devoured her energies. What kind of therapy could help with an addiction to grief? Paulette tried intensive grief therapy because she seemed stuck, unable to move forward in dealing with McKay's death. This therapy was not working because when she left a therapy session, stress or anxiety would trigger a bizarre reaction in her—she would immediately assume a fetal position. She used this posture as a defense measure.

Attempting to free herself from her inner demons, Paulette turned to outside activities in remembrance of her son. She helped to set up The McKay Foundation, established from the donations of individuals sent in to help with the ransom demands. The Foundation was organized to work with funding agencies and schools to educate children about their own personal safety. The Foundation work was important in two aspects: First, Paulette was committed to educating and informing the general public about the dangers of child predators. In this regard she felt the public was ignorant about violence directed towards children. Second, her Foundation work kept her active, out of the house, and engaged with other people.

When Paulette was not out on Foundation work, she confined herself to her home, but the empty quiet solitude of the house was driving her mad. Each day her body declined as the hours rolled by. Addicted to grief, she cried for hours on end. She would look out the window and see cars go by with children in the back seat. They were normal, doing normal things. As Carl went about his work, Paulette asked, "Why can't I get on with my life?"

There were a number of local events planned in remembrance of McKay, and Paulette attended them. A children's library in McKay's name was opened in a corner of a local community college. Paulette went, but a flood of emotions caused her to leave early. It was too emotional. She drove to the nearest Wal-Mart, got a grocery cart, and walked the aisles using the cart as a walker. Wal-Mart was good for her soul.

The Foundation work, however, had a critical drawback. Every event Paulette attended forced her to relive the ordeal. The old wounds never found time to heal over. Every time she spoke about child victimization, visions of yellow tape emerged, and now and again so did a vision of an open back door. Paulette was determined, though, no matter the mental pain, to speak out on children's issues.

A critical problem in the aftermath was time management. Paulette did not know what to do with her time now. Her old schedule had been based on picking McKay up from school, eating yogurt with McKay, helping McKay with his homework, preparing dinner with McKay, reading to McKay, and visiting with McKay about school, football, the leaves on a tree, or anything. This old schedule had filled her days from 3:30 p.m. until 10:00 p.m. Now she had no routine or schedule.

Paulette wandered around the empty house trying to keep herself whole. But she would fall on the floor and curl up in a fetal position, again and again. Her mind floated away. Sometimes she just groaned, sometimes she sat on the floor and rocked back and forth. Her grief nearly consumed her life. But Paulette realized that her actions were so bizarre that she might be committed to an insane asylum. She had to get control, and more intensive therapy was advised. She was encouraged by her local therapist to attend therapy in Tennessee. This was a major step in the recovery process.

In September of 1996, Paulette went to Germantown, Tennessee, for help. All her life she had been independent, and she wanted to participate in therapy for herself, for her self-confidence, for her life. She made her own plans and her own decisions. Most important, she told herself that she was not returning home until the therapists told her she was ready to go home. She made her reservations, packed her bags, and flew to Memphis. Paulette made her way to the rental car area to pick up her car, but she found that she could not sign for the car because during the emotional chaos of the crime and trial she had allowed her driver's license to expire. Little things—it was the little things that had gone by the wayside.

Paulette called Carl, left him a message about her dilemma, and told him she would get to Germantown by taxicab. However, while waiting in the airport she felt uneasy and sensed she was not safe. She read a magazine and then looked up to survey the people around. She noticed a man staring at her. He chuckled when she looked straight at him. He exited the area. Odd, but not unusual because, she thought, you see all kinds of things and people in airports.

Ten minutes or so later she looked up from her magazine and saw the same man staring at her. This time he was standing about eight feet in front of her. Their eyes met, and he chuckled loudly enough for Paulette to hear. They looked at each other for a few seconds, then he turned quickly and walked away at a fast pace. Paulette was frightened. Here she was, away by herself at a vulnerable time, and here was this weird stranger. Was it odd airport behavior? Was it someone connected with Hilton trying to play with her? Her paranoia worked overtime.

The man returned again. This time he stood in front of her until she looked him in the eyes. He laughed and ran out the door. As he ran away, Paulette grabbed her baggage and ran to the taxi stand. She wished that she had contacted the security people. She jumped into a cab and told the driver to head for Germantown.

Paulette directed the driver to some apartments by way of Get Well Road. At the sight of the road sign, Paulette laughed to herself and thought, *I sure hope I do*. The cab stopped in front of the apartments, where a lady was standing. Paulette introduced herself to the woman and found out she was the therapist's wife. Her therapist graciously offered her a condominium, which was within walking distance to his office. The lady helped Paulette with her things, and the cab sped away. As the doctor's wife left, she mentioned to Paulette that there was a notebook on the table in the living room. She advised Paulette to start writing a journal. This was to be her first step on the road to recovery.

While Paulette was working on her journal that night, the phone rang, and the caller asked if she needed a chimney sweep. The caller also asked if she knew a certain witness who had testified on behalf of Hilton during the trial. Horrified, Paulette felt that someone was watching her. This was odd, because no one from home, except Carl, knew that she was in Tennessee. The caller also wanted to know if she was living in an apartment or a house and then hung up.

Terrified, Paulette immediately called one of her sisters, who lived in Jackson, Mississippi, to come and take her away from the place. She also told Carl what happened. Because the man in the airport had not hurt her, there was nothing to be done, so Paulette decided to finish the therapy. Carl informed the local district attorney's office in Conroe. One step forward and two steps back.

The therapy sessions were grueling for Paulette. Therapy began at 8 a.m. with loud music. She heard the "Hallelujah Chorus" every day. There were no coffee or cola breaks or lunch breaks. These therapy sessions were called "goin' sane," and it was difficult to tell just exactly who was sane at this facility. Paulette asked the doctor whether or not any other patients had come to him for help because their children had been murdered. He said, "No," but that he had helped families who had lost a child to drunk drivers. "Rage is rage when a child is lost," he said.

To help deal with her rage, Paulette broke glass jars and bottles. The garbage collector agreed to deal with the glass her friends brought her to break. At night she would stand on her driveway and throw glass jars into the trash can and scream and curse. Paulette knew that she had to vent her rage any way she could in order to get on with her life. It was pure agony. In the meantime, she used her credit card to pay for the therapy. The way off of Get Well Road was costly.

Paulette told the therapist that she read the Bible to discover how Jesus's mother got through the rest of her life after the crucifixion of her son. Her therapist told her to stop worrying and wondering about how Mary got through her life and begin planning how she, Paulette, was to get through her own in a positive manner. Paulette told herself to live her own life because Mary lived her own life. Tough love, but Paulette finally realized that the doctor was right.

She got down to the business at hand of working toward recovery. She wanted to rejoin the human community. In her room, she wrote down the three aspects of therapy she wanted finally to address head-on: her losses and issues in childhood, her loss of McKay, and her anger at being allowed to live while McKay was dead. All three issues triggered her anger, but the combination of the three was staggering and potentially deadly. The three issues were like one-ton pieces of granite that weighed on her shoulders. She had to lose the boulders or be crushed by them. The therapist advised her to work hard in the therapy sessions and take them seriously to get well. The doctor told her, "If you don't bear down and get this behind you, your health will slowly deteriorate and you won't be any good to anyone."

Paulette heeded the doctor's advice and worked hard. She followed his regimen and relived the pain and horror of the crime as he required. She confronted again emotions she had felt about McKay's abduction. She tried hard to feel the last moments of her child. She tried to understand what McKay must have felt when Hilton, a trusted friend tossed him into the trunk. Paulette had to face, as best she could, what McKay felt on that night. The anguish was hardly bearable. But therapy at the Germantown facility helped, and she felt ready to rejoin the world.

Paulette returned home to Texas and spent her days and nights pretty much alone. She painted and played the piano and took care of McKay's pets. Most of all, she heeded her doctor's advice. She seized the moment and made the most of each day. She knew that the old feelings of rage and anger would come and go, but she remained positive and focused on her mission in life. She wanted to teach again and to help children make good decisions.

Paulette's mind was healing slowly, but now her body needed attention. She needed physical therapy, but resisted. At first, she thought she could fix her body herself. She signed up for golf lessons. One lesson involved balancing a golf club on the index finger of her right hand. Even this task was difficult. It took months before she could complete just three holes of golf and many more before she could complete nine, but it was improving. The simple act of walking, hitting a ball, and interacting with others was uplifting.

Eventually, Paulette met with a physical therapist. Her left arm was still weak and wanted to pull up in a palsied position. She began physical therapy twice a week for two-hour sessions. The workouts were strenuous, complete with hot baths, massages, and walking.

The doctor in Germantown supplied Paulette with reading lists.

She read *Man's Search for Meaning, A Grief Observed,* and *Tracks of a Fellow Struggler.* Her reading helped her come to the unacceptable but inevitable conclusion that suffering is part of human existence. She also realized that she had become so engrossed and wrapped up in her own loss that she had given little thought to others who had suffered similar losses at some point in time. Grief and loss are selfish experiences. But Paulette's reading and reflection had helped prepare her for a life without McKay, and she knew she could help others as a way to heal herself.

Victimization pushes many to explore and examine spirituality. Victims often ask themselves, "Why did this happen to me?" or, "Why did God let this happen?" These were questions to which Paulette desperately sought answers. While on a trip to Mississippi, back home to her roots, she listened to a minister preach in a small town park. A lady attending the sermon struck up a conversation with Paulette, and Paulette told the stranger her story. The woman seemed concerned and interested in Paulette and told her that God had not forsaken her, even though she believed He had. The message was important, but so was the messenger. A stranger had spoken with her and connected with her. Paulette was slowly rejoining society one stranger at a time.

On another occasion, she was visiting a friend in New Orleans and they were making their way through a small art gallery. Paulette noticed a piece of paper taped to the window that said, "There is no way to judge the length of one's life." Paulette was searching for messages, and this message helped her re-evaluate her life and how she was going to live the rest of it. She realized that she might not conquer the world but that she could accomplish something each day that was positive, loving, and sincere. The message on the tiny scrap of paper lifted the boulders of grief and anger from her shoulders.

McKay's three dogs and three cats declined, and one died. Paulette felt as if she had lost a part of McKay. Afraid that her life would spiral out of control again, she made a special effort to tend to McKay's remaining pets. She wanted to honor the animals and the role that they had played in her son's life. She wondered if the animals remembered McKay or ever thought of him.

Paulette appeared twice on national television shows (including *Geraldo*) and told her story to the audience. These appearances had their high and low points. The high was the opportunity for Paulette to tell the audience about the kidnapping and murder of McKay by a family friend and to warn her audiences to guard their children. But once she finished her story and the program cut away to a commercial, it would dawn on her that her story was entertainment. She would tell a tragic story to a television audience, but once the audience exited the studio parking lot, they went on with their lives.

There was another fatality for Paulette: Her relationship with Carl deteriorated as a result of the ordeal. Hilton's actions had killed the Everetts' marriage. Everybody focuses on the crime scene and all efforts go toward finding the killer, but murder also has a tendency to damage the inner circle around the victim. Crime statistics account only for the obvious victims—they fail to account for the secondary victims.

Carl was seventeen when he married twenty-one-year-old Paulette. The age difference never bothered them because the two kids from Mississippi shared a bond—both wanted to escape from the Magnolia State. Carl was a fun-loving, simple, down-to-earth guy. In Paulette's mind, he was genuine, not someone with different stories every conversation. When she met him, he was gathering eggs on a farm to earn his way. The two quickly fell in love. They did not have much, but the couple built a solid friendship.

After graduation from college, they discussed having a family, but they agreed to become financially secure first. Carl's work in the oil and gas business provided the security, and Paulette became pregnant. After McKay arrived, they settled into a routine: Carl focused on the business, and Paulette focused on McKay.

Their marriage, like most, had its ups and downs, but the kidnapping and murder of McKay changed everything. The loss of McKay was overwhelming. Carl and Paulette raged over Hilton's betrayal of their child and their friendship. They felt that they had let McKay down by not being at home to protect him. They both felt guilty about what had happened to their son. They swam in a sea of guilt over not seeing the intentions of Hilton. Whenever Paulette looked at Carl, she felt she had let him down as McKay's mother. She could have stayed home and not attended the Amway meeting. Both parents were crushed.

Their collective guilt over the death of McKay turned into a "what if" game, especially for Paulette. She oftentimes asked herself, "What if I had gone to a different university?" or "What if I had stayed home that night?" or "What if I had told Carl *no* when he asked if I would go with him to Amway meetings?" These mind games tore apart their relationship. Paulette even asked herself, "What if Hilton had abducted both McKay and me if I had stayed home?" Questions, more questions, scenarios, and more scenarios pulled Paulette's mind apart.

Like a cancer patient or a recovering alcoholic, she had good days and bad. Good days revolved around Foundation work and having her mind absorbed by details. Bad days were the "what if" days. "What if McKay escaped?" "What if McKay had survived, but his head injury put him in a vegetative state?" She posed these questions to herself nonstop. It was a futile exercise anyway because she knew—she always knew—that McKay was dead.

Carl and Paulette slowly drifted apart. Their conversations became fewer and fewer. Carl moved on. Paulette agonized over their relationship and felt that she had failed not only as a mother, but as a spouse. She felt guilty because she could not handle her own grief or help Carl with his. She could not imagine how a father would feel to have a trusted male friend betray him. Paulette knew how it felt as a mother, but she had no idea what Carl was experiencing.

Paulette described the situation this way: "I was a bystander when McKay was taken away. I mean, I had no control over his fate. I had zero control during the legal battles. I had no control over anything during the investigation or the trial. Worse, I was a bystander to Carl's grief."

At first, Paulette and Carl went round and round together in their circles of grief and personal agony. Over time they moved apart, slowly at first, until their circles stopped touching. They grew so far apart that Carl finally moved out of the house in April of 1998. The two rarely spoke again after that. To this day, Paulette still feels guilty for not being stronger, for not being more masculine in her grief to withstand the agony and mental torture, while keeping her faith and marriage and husband intact.

Paulette had met Wayne Norman, a previous counselor and national salesperson, in the late 1980s. McKay Everett and Wayne's daughter were the same age. Paulette and Wayne married in May of 2001, and Paulette began her new life. Continued therapy, mental and physical, and a new relationship had helped Paulette survive. Though nothing could ever fill the void left by the loss of McKay, Paulette had rejoined the human race.

But there was still one piece of unresolved business. Paulette knew that the day would come, but she did not know when. Until then, that unfinished piece of business remained in a gloomy shadow in the back of her mind. But her daily focus was on the present. "Control what you can and let the rest go," she said to herself. This simple motto helped her move through the days. Returning to the classroom, her professional love, was not out of the question, and, in fact, this became a goal.

Then on February 27, 2003, it came in the mail. It was a normal looking piece of mail, nothing out of the ordinary. The roads of Hilton and Paulette were about to cross one more time. Just as she was emerging from the ashes of September of 1995, she was about to go back in time again.

Chapter 11

Grains of Sand

I was relieved that the trial was over. I felt that justice had been done. I thought I could get on with my life. I also thought about Hilton. What would his life be like now? How would he handle living on death row? Did he think about his own execution? I knew that Hilton would fight hard to live. He never admitted that he murdered McKay. He never showed any remorse for anything. I also knew it would take years for Hilton to be executed. I was prepared for anything because I knew that time was on my side. But in a sense, time was also on his side. As the years went by, so did the interest in my case and situation. It was always in the back of my mind that some judge somewhere would agree with Hilton and he might not be executed. I mean, you never know—anything can happen. I knew that Hilton would fight like heck to stay alive. He had a wife and two children, and these were powerful reasons to fight. I also believed, in my heart, that he was truly evil and that no matter what he said, what crazy legal brief he filed, or how good he behaved in prison, sooner or later justice would be served, and I would be there to see him off. When your son's killer is on death row, you have to be patient.

Time has always fascinated and mystified people. Individuals have written songs about it, poetry has filled books about its intricacies, and mathematicians have long theorized about measuring it. Throughout history people have sought to understand time, to harness it, to divide it into neat sections to give our existence meaning. The inventions of timepieces like water clocks and sundials were early attempts to measure and control time. So, too, was the hourglass, a simple but elegant device that measures time in grains of sand.

The hourglass also symbolizes many a capital murderer's life on death row. Prisoners on death row probably appreciate the meaning of time more than anybody. Each day on the row, a few grains of sand fill the lower compartment of everybody's hourglass. For some inmates, much sand remains in the upper compartment. Their cases are winding their way through the appellate maze up to the federal system and then back to state courts. All these decisions take time. For others, only a few grains of sand remain. Their cases have been decided against them and death dates have been set. Their hourglasses are almost empty—their last meals have been planned.

Hilton Crawford's appellate hourglass had been turned over when he received a death sentence, and the grains began to fall. On Friday, July 26, 1996, Sheriff Guy Williams announced at a Chamber of Commerce luncheon that he had signed the necessary paperwork to transfer Hilton to death row. Crawford, he said, had spent his last day at the Montgomery County Jail. In response to the Sheriff's Department statement, the audience erupted into applause. Hilton, the most hated man in Montgomery County and perhaps even Texas, was on his way to death row. He was now State property. The entire community grieved for the Everett's, but it was over in the minds of many people. It was time to return to normalcy. After all, a new school year was right around the corner. For Hilton Crawford, however, nothing would ever again be normal.

Death row, or *The Row*, is located about fifteen miles east of Huntsville, Texas, in the Ellis Unit, named after O.B. Ellis, a famous director of the Texas prison system. In the 1950s, Ellis single-handedly overhauled the prison system, turning the large penal farms into showplaces of prison management. He died in 1962, but his accomplishments were forever memorialized when a prison unit was named after him.

The Ellis Unit sits on nearly 12,000 acres of land. It opened in 1965, but not before inmate work groups had cleared with large double-bladed axes the virgin pine forests where the prison sits. Once the land had been cleared, the prison was erected.

Ellis, tucked in off a farm road, is barely visible from the highway. The road into the prison is well manicured and tended daily by white-clad inmate yard crews. Right before the prison are the red brick homes of the ranking prison staff. Inmates tend these yards, too. Washed clothing hangs in the sun, and toys are in the yards. To an outsider, the whole scene is rustic and serene, a quiet glade in the deep forest. But something jars the apparent serenity: The prison, which stands adjacent to the red brick homes, is surrounded by a high double fence topped with coils of razor wire. Gun towers dot the fence.

In shape, Ellis resembles a gigantic telephone pole laid on the ground. The pole is the central hallway and the arms radiating off the hallway are the inmate living areas. On one end of the prison is the chapel, topped with a steeple pointing the way for the wayward sheep in the inmate flock. On the other end of the long pole is the gym and yard area. Right before the gym, a favorite place for the inmates to let off steam, are several living areas that angle off the hallway. These cellblocks are death row.

The trip from the jail to death row took less than an hour. As the van snaked its way to Ellis, Hilton could only reflect on his current situation and realize how fast he had fallen from being a man with a nice family, a house with a pool, and a pretty decent life. In Hilton's mind, he was innocent, he was not an evil man. The van turned onto the road leading to the Ellis Unit. Hilton was on State property now, and he was nearing the place that he would call home. The van passed the neat homes of the prison employees and drove past the front entrance to Ellis. Prisoners entered the prison from the back door. Prisons, like houses, have a back door, and here the regulars came and went. Employees and prison visitors entered through a front door.

Prisoners on death row are assigned numbers. Hilton's was #861. This meant that he was the 861st person to be housed on death row in Texas. He was officially checked in, searched, and led to his cell or, in prison parlance, his *house*.

When the door closed behind Hilton Crawford, his mind replayed the events that had occurred over the last two years.

I was at Louisiana Downs, and I met a guy named R.L. Remington. We exchanged business cards, and Remington said he would call me when he came through Houston. He did indeed call me, several times, too, over the next several months. Then out of the blue Remington called me in June 1995 and asked me if I wanted to make some fast money. I told him I didn't really need the money, and he let it go. Well, a short time later he called me again and told me that we could kidnap somebody and make a couple hundred thousand dollars. Best part about it, he said, no one gets hurt. After Remington told me this stuff I started thinking about it and it kept growing on me and growing on me. I was hurting money-wise and it sounded good.

I got a call from Remington at my house; it was on September 10, 1995, around 2 p.m. I told him that I was really hurting for money. He said that he's got an easy way to make money. Well, I told him about a friend of mine named Carl who had money and had a son. I told him about the Amway meeting Tuesday night. Remington said the kidnapping would go down on Tuesday and I was supposed to line up a ransom caller. I told Remington to meet me Tuesday evening around 8:25 at the jewelry store in Conroe that I gave him directions to.

Right after that, I called Irene Flores. She used to work for me. She got arrested on a drug deal and went to the pen. I thought she could do the ransom call. We would pay her, and she would keep her mouth shut. Being to the pen and all that, I thought she was a pretty cool girl. I thought she could handle the pressure. I told her about the deal me and Remington set up and that she would get $30,000 for the call. I told her what to say and to make sure she made the ransom call from a pay phone and then go home. I told her to keep calling the number after 9:30 p.m. until she reached somebody.

I picked up Remington at the jewelry store around 8:20 p.m. He was by himself and he had a duffel bag. He told me a friend dropped him off and headed back to Lafayette. I remember he had on dark blue socks and a dress shirt. He opened the bag and showed me a policeman's shirt. I also saw a hood with drawstrings on it in the bag. I guess we were ready.

On the way over to Carl's house, Remington put on the police shirt and slipped the hood into his back pocket. He told me to keep the car on the street and he would walk up to the door so no one would see him. Remington rang the doorbell and after thirty or forty seconds McKay came to the window in the door and talked to Remington a little bit. Then McKay turned the alarm off and opened the door. I saw Remington lunge at the boy and put the hood over his head. Remington motioned to me and I went up the side driveway to the house.

Remington told me to open up the trunk. I mean, I got as close to that back door as I could. I backed out and we headed out of there, down to Cleveland, and then on to Dayton all the way to Beaumont and I-10. The boy was alive in the trunk. While we were driving, I called Irene on my car phone around 8:35 p.m. and told her that we had picked up the boy and that it was okay to start calling the house. I told her what to say, you know, me and Remington told her to say that we have your son and that he will be well taken care of and that certain steps need to be followed. First, no contact with any law enforcement and second, we wanted $500,000 in cash. We also told her to say that if you contact anyone, you may not see your son again. I tried to call her back to see how it went, but I could not find her. I remember that we told Irene this stuff and we were in Louisiana. Well, around 11:45 p.m., before we got to Lafayette, about twenty miles or so outside the city, a noise started coming from the trunk and it kept getting louder and louder. Remington said to pull off the road, so I did. He got out. I popped open the trunk and I heard a noise like a thump. Remington said the kid would be quiet now. He said he cut the kid's head, but it was not bad.

We drove on in to Lafayette and turned off on a road like we were going to the racetrack, out to Remington Downs. I pulled off the road and we met another car, a '94 burgundy Cadillac. Remington went over and talked to the guy, a white guy, in the car. I thought they were going to take the boy from Lafayette on to New Orleans. Remington said for me to follow that car and I did. We got back on the highway and exited on the Whiskey Bay cut-off and circled underneath the highway and headed west. I think we drove about forty yards on this shell driveway. I was following the car in front of me, and then that car stopped, and so did I.

Remington got real mad and said that the deal had gone bad. I was not happy because I thought they were taking the boy to New Orleans. Remington told me to open the trunk and I did, *and saw a lot of blood in there. His arm and face were covered with blood. His head was cut and he was out. I knew he was hit a couple of times. Remington said that this deal was over. He gets my gun out, which was in the trunk, a .45, and it already had blood on it. Well, Remington grabbed the kid by his legs and the other guy grabbed his arms. They got him out of the trunk.*

Those two guys had him, and McKay never moved, and they threw him in the grass off the road. Remington then shot him twice. And that was it. Remington kept saying we screwed the deal up. He told me to get my ass in my car, get on back to Houston, and not say a word to anyone or he will get my family. I said this was terrible. I just witnessed a murder and these guys just let me go. I have no idea why they let me go.

I drove on out of there fast and checked into a Best Western in Beaumont around 4 a.m. At the hotel, I looked at the bumper and it had blood on it. I looked in the trunk, and there was blood on the mat and on the top part of the trunk lid, the underside of the trunk lid. I tried to go to bed but I did not sleep. I called home around 6:20 a.m. Connie answered the phone and said McKay was missing.

I drove to Billy Allen's place. I told him about a security guard who got hurt bad and bled in the trunk. I lied to him. We ripped out the trunk lining and threw it in a dumpster. I asked Billy to keep the gun for me too. Sometime later I heard on the news that a car with a Crown Motors-Houston sticker on it was seen leaving the house. I took off the sticker as best I could and asked them how to get it off, and the guy told me about some spray. I also took the car through a car wash to clean it all up. I did this after I took my stained clothes to the laundry. I got arrested pretty soon right after that.

On Wednesday, July 31, 1996, Crawford spoke from death row about his role in the kidnapping and murder. Publicly he said he was not a bad man and that he had made a poor decision. He admitted that he had helped kidnap McKay, but he swore that the elusive R. L. Remington was the triggerman. Hilton would not let go of this version of the events.

All capital crime convictions in Texas receive an automatic or direct appeal to the court of Criminal Appeals in Austin. The entire record of Hilton's trial, including all papers, all evidence, and the trial testimony, was forwarded to Austin for review. Hilton's attorneys also filed a brief that outlined errors in the trial, or reasons why the conviction and/or sentence should be reversed.

Death row may confine killers and losers, but most people on the row are not quitters. Hilton Crawford was no quitter, and he was not going to lie down on the gurney and let the State put a needle in his arm without a fight. His plan was, like that of most of his death-row neighbors, to file as many appeals as it took to stave off execution. He doggedly adhered to his version of the crime, which became central to his appellate efforts. But the State of Texas was determined to see closure in Hilton's case. Between 1982 and 1996 (the year Hilton arrived on the row) 107 capital murderers were executed. And the State had all the time in the world. Both sides settled in for a protracted struggle, a war in which there could be only one winner.

Lengthy, epic legal battles between condemned criminals and the State were nothing new. In his effort, Hilton would not be plowing new ground. One of the greatest legal battles waged from death row involved Caryl Chessman, who was convicted of kidnapping and rape in Los Angeles in 1948. Chessman, who received a death sentence for crimes other than murder, maintained his innocence to the end. While on death row, he wrote four very popular books, and his international celebrity gained him pleas of mercy from noted authors, poets, actors, artists, and religious leaders. Those pleas fell on deaf ears, and Chessman was gassed at San Quentin in 1960. Though Hilton had none of Chessman's artistic or rhetorical talent, he fought hard to stay alive.

Shortly after Crawford moved onto death row, the prosecution disposed of the case against Irene Flores. The former convict and accomplice pled guilty to kidnapping and received a twenty-five-year term. Flores was shipped off to prison, eligible for parole in 2008.

In early August of 1996, Crawford's attorneys filed paperwork with the court of conviction seeking a new trial. This initial request was heard in September of 1996 and denied. Also at this time, Judge Fred Edwards assigned Crawford's appellate activities to another Conroe-based defense attorney.

Direct appeals of death penalty cases to the Court of Criminal Appeals are anything but "direct." Hilton received a death sentence in July of 1996. This did not mean that the Austin-based appellate court received Hilton's trial record a few weeks after the trial to review the proceedings. First, Crawford's appellate attorney combed through the entire trial record, from the change of venue application and jury selection to the pronouncement of the death sentence, looking for errors. The appellate strategy at this early point was to locate procedural errors and ask the court to reverse the conviction and/or sentence. On January 20, 1998, following this review, Crawford filed his direct appeal with the Austin court, raising twenty-seven points of error. It was "game on."

Hilton had been on death row for a year and a half before his appeal was delivered in Austin. This is what the capital appellate process is all about: one legal brief at a time. A few grains of sand at a time, no matter how slow the process moved—the players had to have patience. The State, through the Montgomery County District Attorney's Office, filed its reply to Hilton's appeal on June 22, 1998. The State rejected Crawford's appeal, maintaining that no errors had occurred in the trial proceedings.

The case was now in the hands of the Court of Criminal Appeals, a court with eight judges and one presiding judge. This court was, in effect, a mini-Supreme Court. Dozens upon dozens of criminal cases clogged its docket. Much of the business of the court, though, involved death-penalty cases. Oral arguments by both sides in the Crawford's appeal were made before the court on September 9, 1998. One of Crawford's objections dealt with the selection of individual jurors who, his appellate attorney argued, were predisposed to a guilty verdict. Paulette's outburst during the trial was another major appeal issue. Crawford's attorney alleged that the emotions put forth by the victim's mother, in an already emotionally laden trial and in front of the jury, predisposed the jury to convict.

In the meantime, Crawford filed a state *habeas corpus* application in the court where he had been originally tried and sentenced to death. A *habeas corpus* action claims that the conviction and sentence are unlawful and that they violate the defendant's constitutional rights. Crawford filed his application in July of 1998. His state-level *habeas corpus* appeals differed from direct appeals in that he raised thirteen issues based on facts beyond the original trial record. Here, Crawford alleged "ineffective counsel," or that his attorneys were not suitable capital defense lawyers. In August of 1998, the State filed its brief responding to the claims raised by Crawford.

Hilton's appellate attorneys were proceeding predictably and at two levels, with a direct appeal to the Court of Criminal Appeals and a *habeas corpus* application in the original trial court. In November of 1998, after a review of Crawford's claims, the trial court rejected his *habeas corpus* application. Several grains of sand slipped through the bottleneck and bounced around the bottom of the hourglass. Hilton appealed this decision to the Court of Criminal Appeals.

The New Year saw another defeat for Hilton. In February of 1999 the Court of Criminal Appeals affirmed Hilton's conviction and sentence on direct appeal. A few more grains of sand sifted to the bottom of the hourglass. More sand fell through when the Court of Criminal Appeals rejected Hilton's appeal of his initial *habeas corpus* application in his trial court. His case was gaining momentum in the same unfavorable direction that had pushed a number of his death row neighbors toward the death house. In 1997, thirty-seven capital murderers were executed, twenty in 1998. Hilton would see thirty-five more of his neighbors off in 1999.

Most death-row appeals wind up, sooner or later, in front of the United States Supreme Court. After the Texas Court of Criminal Appeals affirmed Hilton's conviction and sentence, he appealed directly to the Supreme Court to hear his case. After he petitioned the Court to hear his case on May 17, 1999, the State then filed a brief in opposition to Crawford's petition.

The Supreme Court refuses to hear most cases in a given year. Hilton's request was no exception, and on October 4, 1999, the highest court in the nation denied Crawford's petition. This ruling caused a number of sand grains to loosen and fall to the bottom of the hourglass. He regarded himself as innocent, and it must have been shocking that nobody could see his side of things. Judges, state or federal, read transcripts, review documents and evidence, and hear oral arguments, but they do not read minds. The wall in his house heard from him, but no one outside of his house would listen.

Having exhausted his appeals on the state level, Hilton next appealed his case in the federal court system. He filed a number of appeals that were similar to his state-level filings. In November of 2000, Crawford's attorneys filed a federal appeal of *habeas corpus,* raising seventeen claims. They were the same claims Crawford had raised in state courts. He argued that he had been deprived of effective counsel because his attorneys were not certified to work on death-penalty trials. He also claimed that he had been deprived of a fair jury selection process and that Paulette's emotional outburst in court had biased the jury. The United States District Court for the Southern District of Texas (Houston) considered Crawford's material and on January 30, 2002, denied his appeal. A few more grains hit the bottom of his hourglass.

Following this denial, Hilton's appellate attorneys wasted little time in asking the same federal district court to reconsider his appeal. His "reconsideration plea" was filed on February 19, and the request was denied on February 28, 2002. In some cases, courts act quickly, and Hilton's case was now moving with all deliberate speed to a conclusion. A few more grains found their way to the bottom.

With these denials in hand, Hilton was running short on options. His next round of appeals made their way out of Texas to the Fifth Circuit Court of Appeals in New Orleans. Hilton's case wound up here because his appellate attorney believed the Federal District Court in Houston had erred in its denial of his appeal. Like two fighters engaged in gladiatorial combat, the State filed paperwork arguing just the opposite, or that the Houston court acted properly in denying Crawford's claim.

The legal gladiators made their oral arguments, and on December 17, 2002, the Fifth Circuit Court of Appeals issued its opinion, denying Crawford's claims. In this ruling, the Fifth Circuit decided that no errors had been made by the State. For Hilton, this decision was a bitter present with which to begin the holiday season. Compounding this news was the fact that two of his death row neighbors were executed that same month. If something dramatic did not occur soon, this would be the last Christmas Hilton would spend on death row. Only a few grains of sand remained in his hourglass.

In January 2003, Crawford's attorney petitioned the New Orleans court to rehear the case. The court denied the request. The appeals and denials were no doubt maddening for Hilton. Briefs and writs were in many respects abstract activities conducted by Hilton's attorneys. All capital cases follow a similar pattern, and time was on the side of the State. New Orleans seemed far away and out of reach. But the legal activity in New Orleans also set in motion legal activities in Texas. On February 11, 2003, the Fifth Circuit denied his rehearing, and the District Court in Montgomery County, the court that heard the original trial, set Hilton's execution for July 2, 2003. Hilton's case was fast moving toward closure. His hourglass had only a few grains left in the upper chamber. Three Texas capital offenders were executed in February of 2003.

Crawford's attorneys filed yet another state *habeas corpus* application in his trial court in February of 2003. They were attempting to start the process all over. But the Court of Criminal Appeals in Austin would hear none of it and dismissed the application as an abuse of the writ.

In June of 2003, Crawford's attorneys once again petitioned the United States Supreme Court to review the new state *habeas* application. On June 23, 2003, the Supreme Court denied Crawford's application and refused to review the case. It was over. Hilton had no other recourse. The sand in his appellate hourglass had all fallen and he had only a few days to live. It was time now to plan his last meal and his last statement.

Hilton had been on death row for seven years and seen over a hundred of his death row mates pack their belongings, take a ride to the Walls Unit, and never come back. He had also seen other condemned criminals come to the row. Every executed prisoner was quickly replaced by another, another, and then another. Prisons are often referred to as having revolving doors because many offenders are released, only to return in a short time. Hilton saw firsthand the revolving door of death row. The only difference was that every time a prisoner left, a new one entered. And those that left never came back. In late June of 2003, Hilton Crawford had one foot in the revolving door.

Chapter 12

Face to Face

I had waited for this day since the trial ended. I knew in my heart that Hilton would be executed. I knew that the judges and courts in Texas and the federal courts would see that there were no errors or anything. Hilton had a fair trial, and it was now time for him to pay for what he did to McKay. He's got it easy. All he has to do is lie there and go to sleep. That's a pretty easy way out, considering how he killed my son. At first I was unsure if I wanted to view the execution. Then I made up my mind to go, not for my sake, but for McKay's. I wanted to see the whole thing through. I wanted to see that evil man go, and then I would know he would never hurt another child. I wondered how I would feel if Hilton looked at me. I wondered if he had anything to say to me. I wondered if he would finally drop the pretense of saying that Remington killed McKay. I wondered if he would be a man and accept responsibility for the whole thing. A lot of thoughts crossed my mind. You know, it's not every day that you prepare yourself to see an execution. It was hard, very hard, but I had to be strong. I had to be strong for McKay. I had to see it through. I wanted justice.

It has been said that "no man is an island," meaning that people, whether they like it or not, are connected in some way. Individuals can never be true isolates or complete introverts. Even Robinson Crusoe needed his friend Friday to survive. It is the nature of the connection between people that warrants concern. The great enigma of the human existence is the need for friendship and companionship. Friends can be a blessing and a curse.

In the catalogue of reasons why people form friendships, betrayal is on the last page in the book. Rarely do people enmesh their lives with those of others, only to undo them later on. This would involve meticulous planning, cunning, and unusual patience. Betrayal with "malice aforethought" is typically the province of espionage agents, narcotics stings, and organized crime investigations. Betrayal by "narcs," informers, plants, and double agents is accepted and necessary to counter illegal activity. In these realms, planned betrayal is legitimate and necessary.

Betrayal in ordinary life by ordinary people is rarely conducted with much advance planning. Something goes wrong in a relationship, a slight is perceived, and the betrayer seeks justice or undoes another for some motive. Whatever the reason for betrayal, betrayer and betrayed often come face to face at the moment of betrayal. Hilton Crawford stuffed McKay Everett in the trunk of a car and bludgeoned him later. McKay knew he had been betrayed. When that trunk lid shut over him, McKay knew his friend, his "Uncle Hilty," had taken complete and deadly advantage of him.

Hilton Crawford, the betrayer, was executed by the state of Texas in July of 2003. He was given a lethal injection while strapped to a gurney in the state's death chamber, and Paulette Norman witnessed the execution. She came face to face with her child's killer.

When Hilton Crawford arrived on death row in July of 1996, the last thing he was talking to the wall about was who would attend his execution. By 2003 the case of the State of Texas vs. Hilton Crawford was winding down. Hilton had nearly exhausted all his legal maneuvers to avoid lethal injection. His good fight had not been enough. Crawford's hourglass was nearly empty—his execution was set for July 2, 2003. Hilton was just another capital offender in the Texas execution pipeline.

In January of 2003, six of Crawford's death row colleagues were put to death. February claimed three more. It looked as if 2003 was going to be a busy year in the death chamber. Between February and June of 2003, Hilton filed additional motions to forestall the inevitable. But Hilton was a gambler, and he certainly knew the odds. The state of Texas was the "house," and all gamblers knew that they can't beat the house. It was just a matter of time before the "house" won.

On February 27, 2003, Paulette picked up her mail. She thumbed through the envelopes and ads. The mail that day, like that on most others, was filled with promotional items, new plans for cell phone users, work-at-home deals, assorted credit card applications, food coupons, magazines, and bills. But one letter caught her eye. It was from the Texas Department of Criminal Justice, the massive state agency that oversees programs for adult probationers, prisoners, and parolees. The agency had done a good job of keeping her and Carl aware of any developments in their case. Paulette tossed the other mail aside and opened the letter and read the contents:

Dear Ms. Everett:

This letter is to inform you that an execution date of July 2, 2003 has been scheduled for Hilton Crawford, #999200.

Please advise if you or other family members desire to view the execution. There are five victim witnesses and three support person slots available, those accompanying you to Huntsville but not viewing the execution.

You may contact Karen Martin of the Attorney General's Office for information on Crawford's appeals process at 1-800-983-9933.

The letter seemed so bureaucratic, so cold and lifeless, a form letter, like a jury summons, and nothing more. Paulette filed the letter away and began wrestling with the idea of attending the execution. She had known this day was coming. It had been in the back of her mind for a long time. Now the execution came to the foreground. Paulette was doing well—she and Wayne were enjoying each other. Everything seemed to be moving along nicely. She would have to weigh all of the consequences before she made her decision.

Victim witnesses to Texas executions do not simply drive to Huntsville, view an execution, get back in their car, and drive home. Although people have viewed executions for thousands of years, in the modern era victim witnesses require preparation and assistance. The Texas Department of Criminal Justice has a Victim

Service Division, which assists victims with, among other things, the execution process. In the jargon of victim advocacy and victim services, executions are regarded as "critical/traumatic" incidents. Paulette received the following materials from the Victim Services Division to help prepare her to view Hilton's execution.

Texas Department of Criminal Justice
Operation Division
Information Sheet

October 2001

A critical/traumatic incident is an occurrence outside the range of normal human experience. It is an extremely stressful situation in which one feels victimized or overwhelmed by a sense of vulnerability and/or lack of control, with possible physical, psychological and/or emotional consequences. Such incidents include witnessing the death of an offender.

Sometimes emotional after shocks or stress reactions appear immediately after the event or a few hours or days later and in some cases, weeks or months may pass. Some common signs and signals of a stress reaction include:

Chills	*Confusion*	*Guilt*
Thirst	*Nightmares*	*Anxiety*
Fatigue	*Poor Concentration*	*Irritability*
Nausea	*Headaches*	*Depression*
Withdrawal	*Loss of Appetite*	*Increased Appetite*

Post Trauma Do's and Don'ts

Within the first 24 to 28 hours following a traumatic incident, remember the following points:

DON'T
· Drink alcohol excessively

- *Use legal or illegal substances to numb consequences*
- *Withdraw from significant others*
- *Stay away from work*
- *Reduce the amount of leisure activities*
- *Have unrealistic expectations*
- *Look for easy answers*

DO
- *Get plenty of rest*
- *Maintain a good diet and exercise*
- *Take time for yourself*
- *Find and talk to supportive peers, partners, and friends (Talk is the most healing medicine)*
- *Expect the incident to bother you*

REMEMBER ... Your emotions are normal reactions to an abnormal situation. It's OK for you to feel whatever you are feeling. You are normal and having normal reactions, don't label yourself crazy. Reoccurring thoughts, dreams, or flashbacks are normal. Don't try to fight them—they'll decrease over time and become less painful. Any prolonged occurrences may indicate a need for professional assistance.

Victim Witness Coordinator
P.O. Box 99 Huntsville, Texas 77340

Critical Incident Stress Management For Family Members and Friends

- *Listen Carefully*
- *Spend Time with the traumatized person*
- *Offer your assistance and listening ear if they have not asked for help*
- *Reassure them that they are safe*
- *Help them with everyday tasks like cleaning, cooking, caring for the family, minding children*
- *Give them some private time*

· Don't take their anger or other feelings personally
· Don't tell them they are "lucky it wasn't worse"
· Traumatized people are not consoled by those statements.
Instead, tell them that you are sorry such an event has occurred and
you want to understand and assist them.

Paulette closely examined the materials, but she still had not decided to attend the execution. The materials stirred her emotions. At times she felt depressed, and at other times she raged in anger at Hilton, the man who had murdered her child. She even thought about scratching and biting that devil who had killed her baby. Despite this range of emotions, her initial decision was to avoid the execution. She thought that watching Hilton die would remain etched in her mind forever, like a black ink stain on a white shirt pocket. She also feared that the execution would replay itself over and over in her mind. Paulette feared that she would always remember Hilton's dying and not McKay's living.

As the date for the execution drew closer, she began to weigh in earnest the positives and the negatives about attending. A "positive" was seeing a monster die; the negative was the potential for flashbacks. She and Wayne watched *Dead Man Walking* to see and understand the process of lethal injection. It seemed like euthanasia, when they put animals to sleep. She thought death by lethal injection looked *easy*.

In March of 2003, Paulette decided to attend the execution. All of her life she had felt threatened by hard events, and she was not comfortable with confronting difficult tasks. For her, attending the execution symbolized the adult thing to do. Adults deal with uncomfortable events, people, and tasks head-on. In her mind not attending the execution would have been childish and cowardly. And she had to see the last act in this tragic play. She had to attend. Carl, on the other hand, decided not to attend.

In an effort to remain connected with the world and to help others, Paulette had returned to the classroom. Despite the tumultuous events, she remained focused on her job, teaching second graders. Once the execution date had been set and the media began contacting her for interviews, teaching helped pass the time and kept some degree of normality in her life. The daily timetable and its regimen also made the time pass quickly. Sometimes her second graders would say, "I saw you on TV last night." She was not sure that her students understood all that was unfolding. This is the way it is for victims, especially for the survivors of violent crime. One self is the victim/ survivor—the object of attention and interest of others. The other self is the "normal" self or, in Paulette's case, the teacher. Balancing the two was difficult for her. It was hard to separate the competing selves. One moment she was teaching second graders to read and to add and subtract; the next moment she was thinking about July 2, 2003.

As the spring semester wound down, the pace of media interviews quickened. The first interview took place on April of 2003 with the *Conroe Courier*. The headline for the article was "Waltz with Insanity," and the focus was on Hilton Crawford. Paulette, who wanted more attention placed on the issue of child victimization, was angry about this slant. Her question was, *Why do we put so much emphasis on the crime and not enough emphasis on how to prevent this crime from happening again and again? It is difficult to sensationalize prevention, but lethal injection brings immediate sensationalism.*

In the process of fighting for his life, Hilton "got religion" on death row. Prison does many things to prisoners—some get meaner, some grow up, some stay the same, and some get beaten down. Every convict adapts to the prison routine and copes the best way he can. Some prisoners cope with incarceration by going the "Jesus route." For some prisoners, the "Jesus route" is real, and they experience a personal transformation, almost a resurrection. For others, "getting right with God" in the joint is a ploy to manipulate the prison staff to use the prison chapel as a meeting place to trade contraband, meet lovers, or look good to the parole board. In prison, everybody has an angle. Hilton "got religion" and even set out on a journey to become a monk. He claimed to minister to other prisoners on death row. Was it real? Was it an angle? Was it a way to cope on death row?

Ever the gambler, Hilton was probably hedging his bets on the afterlife. Conversion was all right, but it was not very dramatic. Becoming a monk was flashy—it was over the top in prison. Hilton's personal stationary had two praying hands in the top-right corner and a quotation from Matthew 6:8 on the bottom of the page. On this stationary, he corresponded with Bill Bieck, a member of the Fellowship Church in Huntsville, Texas. Hilton closed a letter of April 24, 2003, to Bieck with these words:

> If you talk with any chaplain here . . . they will tell you I do have Christ in my heart and that I have always brought Christ to a lot of men here. I have been on my journey to God. I have peace and joy in my heart. The journey has not been easy but I have made it. As my time comes to be executed I see the light.

On June 26, 2003, Bill Bieck and William Hagmaier, from the National Center for Missing and Exploited Children, interviewed Crawford. He reiterated that R.L. Remington was responsible for the death of McKay. Even in his final hours on earth, he never relented or capitulated in his alibi. Hilton stated that Remington told him that child abductions happen often and that no one gets hurt. This line of reasoning seemed odd, given the fact that Hilton was a former police officer and knew the potential for violence in kidnapping. Hilton also told the interviewers that business deals, a serious money crunch, and threats to his family over gambling debts resulted in greed and "poor judgment." Trial testimony had proved this to be true. He said that this situation led to panic attacks when the bills started to mount up. This was true as well. In order to protect Connie, Hilton set up another mailbox so that he could intercept the bills and hide things from her. He also confessed to the kidnapping, but he insistently hung the killing around Remington's neck. It was apparent that he was headed to the grave with his version of events.

On Friday, June 27, 2003, Paulette was interviewed by a Houston-based television station. The interview was short, but it brought home the reminder that Crawford's execution was at hand. Yet it did not seem real. The hours rolled by, and Paulette felt as if she were on the outside looking in. She worked on her breathing and tried to remain calm.

On Sunday, June 29, 2003, Paulette broke with tradition and did not attend church. She stayed at home and rested. She tried to paint but could not concentrate or keep still. She went from her painting area, to her patio, to the piano, to her writing area, and then repeated the process again and again and again. She wondered about Hilton. Mental and physical exhaustion were beginning to take hold of her body.

On Monday, June 30, a reporter from a television station in Beaumont came to their house for an interview. The reporter was fascinated with the story and extracted as many details as Paulette could remember. Two days before the execution, Paulette reviewed and relived the entire tragedy. The interview lasted six exhausting hours. It was helpful to talk about the events and McKay, but now she was worn out. She also received many phone calls from the victim's advocate with the Texas Department of Criminal Justice, Victim Services Division, to see if she needed to talk or had any questions. She kept wondering what Hilton was doing in the short time he had remaining.

Wednesday, July 2, began like any other day at the Norman residence. Paulette and Wayne arose around 6:30 a.m., and Wayne retrieved the newspaper, thinking about his bad back and golf swing, while Paulette prepared breakfast and fed the dog. The weatherman on the television said it was going to be hot. Of course it was going to be hot—it was July in Texas. But Paulette and Wayne made small talk while they ate. Paulette did not feel much like eating. This day began like any other, but it was going to end very differently. Paulette thought about Carl and the good times. She thought about McKay. She thought about Mississippi and how her life had changed since moving to Texas. She thought about Hilton Crawford. Today was different, and tension was slowly building within her.

At 6 p.m. she would see Hilton Crawford, she would come face to face with the man, and one-time family friend, who had murdered her child. The last time she had seen Hilton in person was in July of 1996, at the trial. Tonight Paulette and Hilton would cross paths one more time. Each was about to begin a new journey: Hilton to the afterlife, Paulette to the life after. She wondered how she would react when she saw Hilton again, not in his trial suit, but in his death suit.

In the late morning, Paulette gave an interview to a Houston television station. The reporter asked a number of questions about accomplices Hilton might have had in connection with the kidnapping. After the interview, Paulette and Wayne ate lunch. It was hard to think about eating at this point. But she had two choices: get sick because she did not eat or get sick because she ate. The thought of food made her sick, but she forced down a few bites of a sandwich and some fruit.

The Normans got dressed and prepared to leave, Paulette wore a homemade black pants outfit, and Wayne wore casual pants and a golf shirt. How does one dress to attend an execution? They knew how to dress for weddings, baptisms, funerals, and Christmas parties, but dressing for an execution was beyond their experience.

Paulette and Wayne left their new home in Willis for Huntsville around 2:15 p.m. to meet with a victim advocate from the Texas Department of Criminal Justice—Victim Services Division. The drive to Huntsville took about thirty minutes. The car was quiet, and Paulette stared out the window at the passing scenes as Wayne drove. She noticed cars loaded down with luggage. Trucks moved up and down the highway, taking freight to some unknown destination. That the world should be going about its day-to-day business seemed unnatural, and Paulette felt as if she were in a trance. It was not real. And what was Hilton doing? Was he nervous? Was he saying goodbye to his family and friends? Whom had Hilton invited to the execution?

At the time of his execution, Hilton shared death row with another 420 condemned men. Executions in Texas are scheduled for 6 p.m., and to keep his date with death, Hilton was driven by van from death row in the early afternoon to the "death house" in the Walls Unit in Huntsville. The death house was a small red brick building in the northeast corner of the prison. It was the same building where the old electric chair had conducted its business.

Hilton entered the death house door and saw another door on his right—this was the place where his witnesses and McKay's survivors would view his execution. Behind that door were two small rooms separated by a partition for the witnesses. Straight ahead a few steps away was a second door, the entrance to the old death row cells. To his right was the first cell, which functioned as a shower. The second cell was covered with heavy black screening and was used for attorney visits. After being searched and fingerprinted, Hilton was taken to a third cell. He was visited shortly thereafter by the warden and chaplain. The warden visited each death-house inmate to ascertain his or her frame of mind, to determine whether or not the condemned was going to fight the staff, to discuss legal issues and disposition of the body and personal property, and to ask whether or not the inmate had a final statement. The condemned also selected his or her last meal. Hilton's final moments were now at hand. The clock on the wall slowly ticked away.

Paulette experienced flashbacks of the trial, and, oddly, she remembered not seeing Connie Crawford in the gallery. The closer the Normans got to Huntsville, the louder and louder the car tires seemed to get as they rolled over the highway. Paulette could feel the tires turning faster and faster and faster. A few miles south of Huntsville, rising above the pine forest like a lighthouse, is a large statue of the Texas hero Sam Houston. As they passed the statue, Paulette finally understood that she was moving closer and closer to Huntsville and she really was going to watch Hilton Crawford's execution. She thought about the advice from the victim's advocate and breathed deeply and tried to relax.

Meanwhile, Hilton informed the warden that he was going to offer no resistance—he would "go down" quietly. What was the point in fighting? Hilton was sixty-four years old. He was no brawler or thug. Of course he was going to go down quietly. The vast majority of condemned Texas killers go quietly. Besides, a football team of prison security officers is on hand to drag reluctant killers to the death chamber. Fighting was not an option for Hilton.

For his last meal Crawford ordered twelve beef ribs, three enchiladas, chicken fried steak with cream gravy, crisp bacon sandwich, ketchup, a loaf of bread, cobbler, three cakes, three root beers, French fries, and onion rings. Hilton was showy in life, and he made sure he was going to be flashy on the way out. It was over the top, but that was Hilton. He liked to play to the crowd. Crawford probably wanted everybody to remember him.

As Wayne and Paulette neared Huntsville, Paulette thought about the execution process and lethal injection. She thought that Hilton was going to die a most embarrassing death. She believed lethal injection was humane, but embarrassing. She thought about Hilton being stretched out on the gurney like a sick dog at the veterinarian's office waiting to be put to sleep and awaiting the unknown. Paulette was also very angry at the man who had taken her child. She tried to find the words to describe Hilton. At first she thought he was a sociopath, but *no*, he was in reality a psychopath. Psychopaths are amoral and have no regard for others. She remembered this from her college days. Then she thought about Crawford in much simpler terms.

"In the car on the way to Huntsville I could see Hilton's face in the window and I thought," said Paulette later, "that he was a nut, an idiot."

Paulette looked at Wayne and broke the silence: "Hilton was a really stupid criminal. You know that?"

Wayne, not taking his eyes off the road, replied, "You're right, you're absolutely right. It's a funny thing about cops—they make the worst criminals. You'd think they know about getting caught and the ins and outs of investigations and all that. It was really stupid."

The silence returned, and Paulette's feelings turned harsh toward Hilton's children. She hoped that his children were having psychological difficulties as they awaited their father's death at the hands of the State. She hoped that his children were embarrassed. Paulette hoped that because of their father's actions, Hilton's children would reevaluate their own lives and make good decisions. Victimization changes people's thinking about many things.

But most of all, Paulette thought and dreamed about McKay, and how much she missed him and how lonely she was without him. She thought about what McKay would have done had she been kidnapped. In the end, Paulette tried to think of the positive experiences that she had shared with McKay. "It was so stressful, and I wanted to think of McKay. I made my mind see McKay. I remembered the mimosa trees too. I made my mind flash these pictures in my memory." Paulette said afterwards, "I wanted to focus on McKay living, not Hilton dying."

The memories of McKay were intensely painful because the photo album in her mind stopped in 1995. The family album would forever remain half filled. There would be no high school football pictures or snapshots of proms, no tuxes, no limousines filled with laughing kids, no graduation pictures. Murder kills memories, it eliminates futures, and it freezes family albums in time.

Wayne drove the car into the driveway of the place where they were to meet the victim-service staff. He maneuvered the car into a parking spot and Paulette was jerked back to reality. They were across the street from the Walls Unit, and a hundred yards away from the Death House. They had arrived to see the end. Hilton had arrived too.

Wayne and Paulette exited the car and walked up to the building for their 3:30 p.m. meeting with the victim advocates. The meeting took place in the old prison director's residence just west of the prison.

The meeting with the victim-service staff was very informative and matter-of-fact. They were informed about the whole execution protocol and what to expect. Paulette and Wayne also watched a video that detailed the execution process, the death chamber, and the witness viewing room. They were also briefed about the possibility of protesters being present in front of the prison, and about how the lethal drugs might affect the condemned's body. The meeting with the victim advocate lasted until 5:15 p.m., and the group walked across the street to the prison. The execution process had begun.

As they walked across the street Paulette did, in fact, see several protestors on the corner. The protesters whispered, and some held signs that decried state-sanctioned murder. One sign said the governor was a murderer. A bearded professor from the local university, in a straw hat and sandals, stood quietly nearby and held a lit candle.

Paulette had no ill feelings towards the protestors. She only wondered why they wanted to remember Hilton as the "victim" and not her poor child.

The group made its way up the walk alongside the old prison. They were right near the wall that surrounded the place. The wall kept the prisoners in, but it could not stop the smell of the evening meal from drifting over. It was an awful odor. Paulette wondered what Hilton was eating. She also asked herself "How could anyone facing execution eat?"

Halfway up the sidewalk, a victim's advocate told Paulette, "You see those guards in the guardhouse. They are sharpshooters and can pick a fly off an Oreo." They walked up the steps to the front door.

The group entered the old prison, and Paulette saw nothing

but bars. They made several turns and entered another room. Here they could pause for a moment, eat cookies, and have something to drink. They talked about whatever came to their minds. They did not go over or retell any of the execution procedures or rituals.

This meeting room was on the second floor of the prison. Paulette looked out the window and saw several protesters with signs opposing the death penalty. Looking away from these people, she saw about fifty other people who were there to show support for the execution of a child murderer. She saw a friend of hers go up and talk to the protesters. Later she found out that her friend had asked the protesters what they knew about McKay and the life he once lived. The friend received no reply.

For Paulette these few minutes preceding the execution were a respite from the event soon to happen. She had already been informed about the execution procedures and what to expect. She had absorbed a mind full of details about the end of Hilton. Paulette's goal was to witness the execution. The details of that event were numbing. Wayne and Paulette were also informed that there would likely be no stays of execution. The execution would proceed.

Accompanied by two victim's advocates from TDCJ-Crime Victims Unit, Paulette and Wayne walked through a maze of bars on the way to the Death House, a self-contained small building attached to the inmate visitation room. Prior to McKay's murder, the prison system and the Death House had been figments of Paulette's imagination. These were places that few ordinary people ever came to experience. Prison possibly, but the Death House was clearly out of the ordinary. Paulette thought about the stupid decisions made by Hilton Crawford and Irene Flores that would provide her with a personal tour of the Death House.

Wayne and Paulette were informed that five members of the media would also witness the execution and that these individuals would be divided between the victims' side and the offender's side. Paulette thought, *It is like a wedding, one side for the groom's family and the other side for the bride's.* But an execution gurney stood in place of an altar.

Paulette was reminded that if she said anything or did anything provocative during the execution, she would be removed from the viewing area. Any outburst also would jeopardize the victim witness viewing policy and could harm the procedure for future victims. The burden was heavy. Paulette was determined to be a good victim.

A prison security officer led them to the Death House. Wayne and Paulette were pat searched before they entered the victim viewing area. They entered the witness viewing room a few minutes before 6:00 p.m. Thick glass and steel bars separated them from the gurney. The actual room with the gurney was very small. It was painted a light green. Paulette's eyes immediately focused on the person in the next room. It was Hilton, and he was already strapped to the gurney and his arms were outstretched with IV tubes leading to the room with the two-way glass. He was ready.

Hilton lay on the gurney with his head pointing west and his feet pointing east. A microphone was suspended above his head. Paulette stepped closer to the window. Wayne and the others surrounded Paulette, and Wayne pressed against her to hold her up in case she fainted or became emotional. The last thing that anyone wanted was to have Paulette removed at that crucial time.

The warden was standing near Hilton's head, and the prison chaplain stood near his feet. Both officials would be with Hilton throughout the execution. Paulette thought it was nice that Hilton would not be alone at his death. He had not offered McKay the same courtesy. Hilton's head was at the window by Paulette. She wondered what he was thinking and feeling. The ceiling was very low, and it seemed as if they were in a box. Despite the obvious tension, Hilton appeared to be very calm. He was so calm that Paulette thought he was sedated. Just then he turned his head, and he looked right at Paulette. When he saw her, he nodded and smiled. His smile reminded her of bodies she had seen at funeral homes. He was trying to be calm and gentle. Paulette also thought his behavior was carefully planned, that it was his way of manipulating the event. She offered no smile in return.

The silence was broken when the warden asked Hilton if he had any last words. Hilton responded:

> Yes sir. First of all, I would like to ask Sister Teresa to send Connie a yellow rose. I want to thank the Lord Jesus Christ for the years I have spent on death row. They have been a blessing in my life. I have had the opportunity to serve Jesus

Christ and I am thankful for the opportunity. I would like to thank Father Walsh for having become a Franciscan, and all the people from all over the world who have become my friends. It has been a wonderful experience in my life. I would like to thank Chaplain Lopez and my witnesses for giving me their support and love. I would like to thank the nuns in England for their support. I want to tell my sons I love them. I have always loved them. They were my greatest gift from God. I want to tell my witnesses—Tannie, Rebecca, Al, Leo, and Dr. Blackwell—that I love all of you and I am thankful for your support. I want to ask Paulette for forgiveness from your heart. One day, I hope you will. It is a tragedy for my family and your family. I am sorry. My special angel, I love you. And I love you, Connie. May God pass me over to the Kingdom's shore softly and gently. I am ready.

When Hilton stopped talking, he was asked if he had anything else to say. He said, "No." There was only silence. The silence was broken by chanting from the room next door. Crawford's religious teachers were praying for him. The warden then nodded, which was the signal to the people in the next room, the people behind the two-way mirror, to administer the lethal injection. Hilton lay there and waited. Death was on the way. It was creeping slowly, methodically, through the IV tube towards his body.

The first drug to enter his body was sodium pentothal. This was same drug that dentists used to prepare patients for oral surgery. Sodium pentothal was given to Hilton to quickly render him unconscious and insensible to pain. The dose was three grams, or ten times the normal amount of the chemical used in minor surgeries. The drug moved through the IV tube into his arm.

The drug was fast acting, and Hilton went to sleep in less than sixty seconds. The second drug pumped into his body was pancurium bromide, used to relax his chest muscles and diaphragm and stop his breathing. His body was shutting down. On the outside he looked calm and in a deep sleep, but inside there was a fight. His brain was telling his body parts, "No, no, don't go to sleep. Come on, wake up, wake up, you gotta wake up!" It was too late—Hilton was dying, and his brain could not change the effects of the drugs.

The final drug, potassium chloride, was then pumped through the IV tube into Hilton's arm and bloodstream. Potassium chloride caused cardiac arrest. All three drugs were administered in about five minutes.

As the drugs entered Hilton's body, Paulette watched for signs of death—or anything, for that matter. What did death look like? She saw his chest rise and slowly fall. She was not sorry that he was dying. She shed no tears. In preparation for the execution, the prison staff had explained that one of the lethal drugs would cause the chest to expand. The witnesses were told to listen for a snorting or a gurgling sound or a cough or hissing sound. She heard none of these sounds. She stared at his chest and noticed that Hilton's breathing was steady, but growing more shallow. She noticed a faint tinge of gray-blue coming over his skin. This was not her imagination. She looked at his body as a child would, and as an adult would. In a split second her mind said, like a child, "He's turning blue!" Then the adult in her mind said, "He's dying."

Before the execution started, Wayne told Paulette to squeeze his hand very hard if she wanted to say something or do something that was inappropriate or something that could have them removed from the viewing room. Paulette squeezed Wayne's hand hard the entire time. Although she appeared restrained on the outside, she was irate on the inside. When she heard the chanting and praying in the next room, she wanted to bang on the walls at Hilton's viewers and ask them why in the world they were praying for a madman. She was amazed that anyone could sympathize with a child killer. She also wanted to jump through the glass window and scream. She wanted to act crazy. She wanted to jump through the glass and stab Hilton with an ice pick 10,000 times for what he had done to McKay. Remaining poised and rational was anything but normal. But Paulette kept squeezing Wayne's hand. She would be a good victim.

The time passed slowly. It seemed like forever. Paulette knew, however, that with each passing second, Hilton was dying. He never flinched, not even a minor twitch of his head, hand, or foot. He lay completely motionless. Paulette wondered if Hilton's insides were screaming and begging for life. She hoped and prayed his brain was going crazy.

A medical attendant entered the room and checked for any

vital signs. By this time Hilton was a definite shade of blue, the color of death. The medical attendant pronounced Hilton Crawford dead at 6:19 p.m. Paulette thought, *Thank God, he is gone and won't harm another child*. The ritual was over.

The prison system maintains an "execution recording," or official log of events in every execution. The following information was the recording of events for Crawford's execution.

EXECUTION RECORDING

OFFENDER: Crawford, Hilton #999200
EXECUTION DATE: July 2, 2003

TAKEN FROM HOLDING CELL
TIME   6:01

STRAPPED TO GURNEY
TIME   6:03

SOLUTION FLOWING
RIGHT HAND/ARM   6:04
LEFT HAND/ARM   6:09

LAST STATEMENT
TIME   6:11

LETHAL DOSE BEGAN
TIME   6:14

LETHAL DOSE COMPLETED
TIME   6:19

Hilton Crawford, the second oldest capital offender in Texas, the former police officer, father, and one-time baseball coach, was dead five minutes after the lethal cocktail of drugs entered his body. He was the seventeenth capital offender executed in 2003.

After Hilton was pronounced dead, Paulette's body began to react to the stress of holding in everything that she wanted to do and say to Hilton. Wayne and the others had to hold her up. She thought that this was not what it should be like for victims. She felt cheated. She could not be herself and say what she wanted to say. She had to be careful, to exercise caution in word and deed. She felt confined. Yet Hilton, the kidnapper and child murderer, was allowed to speak his mind before the media. Hilton was allowed to present his side of the events, in his soft words and soft voice. He tried to come across as the "guy next door." Paulette thought that it was odd for the media and those who befriend death row killers to stand in awe of monsters and believe that, strapped to the gurney, they can become changed and redeemed persons.

The Normans were led away by a prison security officer to a room where they could talk about the events with a chaplain. Paulette's body was racked with stress. She felt as if she walked in slow motion. The stress resulted from her focused, determined restraint while watching her child's killer freely express his emotions. In her mind, the system was abusive to victims. Victims were expected to do too much to keep the criminal comfortable. In turn, their forced restraint causes more physical and emotional trauma for the victim.

Paulette was led across the street to a small press conference. She read a written statement:

> Today marks an end to a long Chapter 13 in a book of 20 chapters—the story of how my son's life was taken from him. Today the justice system is doing their job. The wheels of justice grind slowly, but they grind. I deeply miss McKay. My dream was for McKay to grow to be a man with a servant spirit. My dream was shattered by those who dreamed of reducing debt and purchasing a new home. The McKay Foundation was established when McKay did not come home. The McKay Foundation works to help boys and girls be safe at home, at school, and on the playground. I remind myself often that my choices determine my destiny regardless of how the choices of others impact my life. Thank you.

Then Paulette answered a few questions from the press. She said that Hilton's last statement meant nothing to her. She believed that Hilton, even until the very end, tried to detach himself from the murder of her child. Hilton never uttered any words of remorse at the end and never mentioned McKay. When asked if she forgave Crawford, Paulette said, "Forgiveness is God's job."

Hilton's execution was a sobering, somber experience. It was difficult for Paulette to comprehend and impossible for her to convey her true feelings, emotions, and mental state to anyone. Paulette had experienced the brutal murder of her son. She had also seen the execution of the perpetrator of the horrible deed. Few people in American society are so experienced in grief, loss, survival, and violence.

A Mexican restaurant in Huntsville agreed to section off part of its interior for Paulette's friends and supporters to visit with her. They met, hugged, made small talk, and ate dinner. Some friends stood away from her and stared at her. These friends told Paulette later that they did not know what to say to her or how to act in front of her. Paulette took this in stride because she knew that few people ever experience the rigor and emotions in the aftermath of an execution. When it was time to leave the restaurant, a friend had to help Paulette to her car because she had difficulty walking. The stress and anxiety of the execution had not dissipated.

On the way home, Wayne asked Paulette about her feelings. Her childlike side emerged, and all she talked about was the blue color of Hilton's skin. She was amazed at how blue his body had turned as the result of the lethal drugs. To this day, the blue color of his skin still amazes her. She also could not erase from her mind the memory of how peaceful Hilton's death really was. He merely went to sleep. She wondered how often Hilton had thought about his execution before the event. Did he see a video about the process? Did he take a field trip to the death chamber? How was Hilton prepared to die?

Now that Crawford was dead and the case officially closed, Paulette reflected on the death penalty. She had been in favor of capital punishment before McKay was murdered, during the trial and the appellate process, and at the execution itself—her stand remained unchanged after the execution. Viewing the execution was a good thing for Paulette; she said, "Seeing the execution with my own eyes convinced me that Hilton Crawford was dead and gone. I witnessed it for myself. Didn't have to hear it on the news or read it in the papers."

But the current mode of execution was, in Paulette's opinion, very humane, too humane, compared to what Hilton had done to McKay. "I just wish it had been more painful for him. In my opinion, he got off easy. He went to sleep." The murder was a brutal act; the execution by lethal injection was dignified. Hilton had a last meal and made a final statement. To an extent, he had some say in the final minutes. He was able to control his exit from this world and to control how the world would remember him. Victims like McKay were not offered the choice to make a final statement, and they had no time to say goodbye to anyone. Victims have no control over their final exit.

When Wayne and Paulette returned home, they turned on the lights, turned on the television, and watched the evening news. They went to bed, but it took a long time for them to fall asleep. Wayne awoke early the next morning and went out to retrieve the paper. He winced as he bent over to pick up the paper and wondered if his golf swing would ever come around. He really wanted to get back on the course again. Paulette arose, still stiff but getting better. The couple talked about traveling and relaxing. They also discussed plans to attend a local Fourth of July parade. After much consideration, they decided to decorate their golf cart with The McKay Foundation banner and participate in the local parade. Paulette attended the parade the next day to show people that she was not homebound or despondent. Most important, she wanted to show people that she was alive and in charge of her life. She did not want people to pity her.

After the parade, Wayne and Paulette traveled and spent most of the summer out of town. The school year was approaching fast, and Paulette needed to be ready to teach her second graders. It was back to normal, but how could anything ever be normal again?

Chapter 13:

It Is Done

After the execution, I was so tired and worn out I could not sleep. I was exhausted after the trial, but standing there watching Hilton die was absolutely the most physically draining experience I have ever had. I can't even find the words to describe it. The best part about it was that it was now over, it was finally over. It was done. Hilton was dead, finally. Not closure or any other fancy word, but simply over. The execution was the last remaining part in this whole story. The execution was also the last connection to McKay. For eight years his loss consumed my life. I even lost my husband. But it was done now and I had to pick up and move on. I had to make a life, to live a life, without my beautiful son. I had to do something so he would not be forgotten. I wanted to make sure that McKay was remembered. I decided to live. He lives because I live.

Collateral damage was a phrase coined in the early 1990s by the American military to denote accidental damage to buildings and structures. The phrase also refers to accidental killings, usually of civilians or non-combatants, in a war zone. For example, a laser-guided bomb blows up an enemy weapons depot, but the explosion also kills and maims a number of patrons at a nearby café. This euphemism, which has now filtered into American culture, basically means damage that was unintended, unexpected. Collateral damage is also a useful phrase or concept that can improve our understanding of the consequences of violent crime, especially as it relates to Paulette Everett-Norman.

In 2004, there were an estimated 5.5 million personal crime

victimizations in the United States. Such personal crimes—which include robbery, assault, and sexual assault—account for roughly one-quarter of all crimes committed in our society. Personal or violent-crime victimizations are vicious, life-threatening, and life-changing events. Being a victim of personal crime has consequences far beyond the criminal act. The damage done has collateral effects that endure for months, years, and, for some victims, a lifetime. Violent crime impacts the body, mind, and spirit of victims. Paulette and Carl have grieved for the loss of McKay since 1995. There is no greater form of suffering in the catalogue of human emotions than that from losing a child.

Current textbooks and research monographs on victimization offer the latest information on the effects and aftermath of victimization. Research has demonstrated that many victims remain angry at the perpetrator for years and have to take time off work as a result of victimization. Many victims go through life feeling isolated and alone. Worst of all, victimization negatively affects relationships between the victim and their family and friends.

We also know that many victims and survivors, especially those of violent crime, experience depression, flashbacks, hostility, rage, sleep disorders, paranoia, and post-traumatic stress syndrome. These concepts and words sound scientific and impressive—they represent the vocabulary of academics and therapists. But these words are sterile and cannot convey the inner turmoil that victims feel. Victims feel totally devastated, and no one else can speak for them or walk in their shoes. Only they know what it is like to be a victim.

The kidnapping and murder of McKay Everett set off a chain reaction of events akin to casting a pebble into a still pond. Some ripples were easily perceptible; others moved beneath the surface and could not be seen. The collateral affects of the events that unfolded between September 11, 1995, and September 17, 1995, have remained with Paulette Everett-Norman to this day, almost ten years after the death of McKay. Paulette must be recognized as a multiple victim—a victim of betrayal, a survivor of a horrible murder, the survivor of a lost child. Crime victims, especially violent-crime victims, are not just "victims" in some abstract sense. The criminal event attacks and impacts the victim's body, mind, and spirit.

Paulette was forty-five years old when she experienced a stress-induced stroke due to Hilton Crawford's decision to abduct and murder McKay. She lost temporary movement of her left arm and right leg. Though recovered, she continues to this day to take medication for the ailment. She watches what she eats and monitors her weight daily. She also engages in some exercise every day. It took her three years of diligent physical therapy, physical training, and speech work to reestablish her mobility and speech. The stroke slowed her speech and delayed her ability to process information at the same speed as that of other individuals. She knew what she wanted to say, but could not "get it out" until after long pauses. The worst part about the situation was the fact that during her pauses to sort out the prior information, everyone else moved on with the conversations, and then she would blurt out her thoughts or answers when the words reached her mouth. Paulette was aggravated and embarrassed by her slow speech.

Witnessing the execution was catharsis for Paulette, a watershed event in her life. The execution set her free. Several months after witnessing the event Paulette said,

> Seeing the execution firsthand was a baby-step in my life. It was one event among a million. I do have some flashbacks of the execution, like when Hilton turned his head towards me and our eyes met, but these images are not upsetting to me. I guess I'll always see these images. The images are also interesting to me as well. It's puzzling when you think about it, especially when I think about how McKay died. Hilton was allowed to ease through death's door. Hilton pushed the door open and walked on through. McKay was beaten, shot, and shoved through death's door. That's the big difference. It's easy to see but so hard to understand why. I've got perspective on the execution now. The execution doesn't occupy a central place in my life. It was a few moments in a lifetime.

All the drama and coverage of executions in our society involves the offender. The media provides images of the placard-holding crowds in front of prisons where executions take place to suggest a certain "blood thirstiness" about American society. The images of the crowd stir up images of the crowds eagerly watching gladiatorial combat in the Roman Coliseum. Endless reports document the last days and moments, the calls to parents, and the last words. We are even provided with the details of the condemned's last supper. In short, executions are about the executed. Yet death opened the door of life for Paulette. Maybe it took Hilton's death to help Paulette live. Prior to the execution, Paulette was trapped in the role of a victim. As long as Hilton remained alive, people could identify with or see her only as a victim. As time passed, and the appellate process wound down, she was less a victim and more a survivor. Better to be a survivor than be typecast a victim in our society. For Hilton, execution was the final chapter in his book, while for Paulette the execution was just another chapter in her book of life.

Getting past the "Hilton chapter" in her life was a prime motivator for her to attend the execution. Her inner strength was building, and the belief that his death would release her from the past helped Paulette engage ordinary life in a confident manner.

It has been over three years since Paulette witnessed the execution of Hilton Crawford. Yet the physical consequences of the crime, trial, drawn-out appellate process, and final justice remain central elements in her life. It has not been easy to completely bury the past. The crime-induced aches have been intensified by the aging process. Something aches in her body all the time, and reliving the crime and all its surrounding issues only serves to cause the aches to linger. To this day, she has relapses of slow speech and slow physical movement. Her left eye often quivers and has blurred vision. If she feels particularly stressed, her right eyelid refuses to open. She has learned to live with and adjust to these "minor" inconveniences by finding a quiet place and relaxing for ten to fifteen minutes until the problems subside. These effects are still apparent nearly a decade after the crime. Wayne Norman, her husband, has emerged as a constant source of support.

Some people who read this account will no doubt suggest that Paulette's current physical issues are psychosomatic. Others might even suggest that Paulette uses her physical ailments as a ploy to garner attention. That's the thing about being a crime victim—only the victim can appreciate the physical aspects of being a survivor. Are these physical ailments real, or are they self-induced coping mechanisms? It does not make any difference. If a person believes something is real, then whatever is at issue is real in its consequences. Every ache is a daily and persistent reminder of her child's murder.

To a large degree, the body can be reshaped, but the mind is a very different matter. Before September of 1995, Paulette was a trusting person. Since September of 1995, she trusts no one. Today, she takes time to study people. She examines each person she comes in contact with. She studies his face, words, and actions. She scans each person for anything that appears to spell "hidden agenda." These actions, some would say, are classic symptoms of paranoia, but they have helped Paulette to become more confident about taking care of herself. She even took firearms training and is licensed to carry a handgun. Though this response is extreme, Paulette reserves the right to protect herself by her own means. The emotional costs of the crime have indeed altered the way in which she sees others, but her experiences are "normal" when compared those of other victims.

When traveling by plane or walking through shopping malls, Paulette notices what other people are reading and saying. She listens to their words. She takes particular notice if she hears someone talk about or discuss their efforts to help children. Recently, she was on an airplane, and the man sitting next to her began talking with her about grant writing, children, and efforts to help children. They had a long conversation. They exchanged contact information; however, her fellow traveler never contacted her. She tried to contact him. If he were really interested in helping children, he would have contacted her. People, she has learned, deceive each other all the time, even on innocent plane rides. Will she ever trust again? She is on guard, like a night watchman, all the time.

The body can be reshaped, and the mind can be disciplined to allow daily functioning. In many respects, getting by and grinding out an existence can be readily achieved. The long-term consequences of violent crime on the spirit are altogether another matter. Eliminating the will to survive, the will to carry on, and the will to achieve other successes or contributions to life is certain emotional death. Some crime victims have their spirits quashed and, in therapeutic jargon, they resort to self-medication and become alcoholics. Some consume mind- and spirit-numbing pills to survive, and some survivors even resort to suicide. Most victims survive, but each takes a different path. Life is a daily struggle.

As Paulette greets every day, she feels angry that she is still alive. The ultimate struggle was learning how to get through the moments of the day without McKay. To smell his clothes, to see his room and bed, to rock in the rocking chair where she sat with him, and to hear the silence of an empty house were only a few of the shocks that she had to confront each day. Collectively, these shocks nearly demolished her spirit and will to live. She became consumed with absolute anger. She was full of rage, and though the execution has helped calm these feelings, Paulette still harbors intense hatred toward Hilton Crawford. Her mind still allows thoughts and images of September 12, 1995, to re-emerge. Memories of the week from hell enter her mind when she least expects them to. She revisits those old memories but does not allow them to consume her very existence.

To help keep the spirit of McKay alive and to will her own spirit to keep on living, Paulette returned to the world of work. It was more than a matter of money. She needed to rejoin the world and take steps to take care of herself.

Paulette taught two writing classes for one semester at a local community college. One class was at 7:00 a.m., and the other was at 7:00 p.m. on the same day. The routine was needed, but the physical grind was too much. She tried to get a job at a local furniture store. The owner, however, knew who she was, and he knew the notoriety surrounding McKay's murder and Crawford's execution. The store owner thought that she was joking about working for him because having her in the store would be a "downer" and people would not purchase his merchandise. He did not hire her. She also tried to secure employment with a local car dealership. The owner gave her several interviews but persuaded her not to take the job because she would be outside on the car lot in the heat. It was good advice, and Paulette declined the offer. She decided to return to teaching.

Returning to the classroom filled a large void in her life. Paulette had always enjoyed teaching children to read, write, sing, use microscopes, paint pictures, and do arithmetic. Teaching children also provided her the opportunity to think about how our society might better protect them. Paulette set about developing a safety curriculum for children. She has become an outspoken proponent of teaching children academic skills as well as life skills. Paulette believes that children need to be taught how to be safe, to protect themselves. Her spirit is kept alive by taking steps to improve the survival skills of children.

Paulette has been so committed to educating children about personal safety that she and several colleagues with the McKay Foundation applied for and received a grant from the U.S. Department of Education to develop a child safety curriculum for fourth-, fifth-, and sixth-grade students. The curriculum was being field-tested in a Houston elementary school. The results of the course evaluation are positive, so Paulette hopes to work with the Department of Education to disseminate the curriculum nationwide. This activity helps to keep her spirit alive and functioning.

Paulette recently stated, "The final chapter won't be written until my life is over. My hope and my goal in the here and now is to leave something behind for children that will lessen their chances of being victimized."

We ask ourselves, "Why did McKay die?" We also ask, "Why does any child have to die?" On August 22, 1924, the famous defense attorney, Clarence Darrow, pled for the lives of child killers Nathan Leopold and Richard Loeb. Part of his plea to the judge in 1924 has a bearing on Paulette's child-safety work. Darrow said to the judge:

> And I want to say that the death of poor little Bobby Franks should not be in vain. Would it mean anything on account of the death, these two boys were taken out and a rope tied around their necks and they died felons? Would that show that Bobby Franks had a purpose in life and a purpose in his death? No, your Honor, the unfortunate and tragic death of this weak young lad should be something. It should mean an appeal to the fathers and the mothers, an appeal to the teachers, to the religious guides, to society at large. It should mean an appeal to all of them to appraise children, to understand the emotions that control them, to understand the ideas that possess them, to teach them to avoid the pitfalls of life. Society, too, should assume its share of the burdens of this case, and not make two more tragedies, but use this calamity as best it can to make life safer, to make childhood easier and more secure, and to do something to cure the cruelty, the hatred, the chance, and the willfulness of life.

As her new chapter in life, Paulette has embraced the idea that people should work together to make life easier and less tragic for children. In this way, McKay did not die in vain. In this way, education can empower the children who are still with us.

Despite the success of her Foundation activities, Paulette's spirit to remain alive is assaulted daily. Nothing—no matter how many good works are done on the behalf of children or adults—can erase the ever-present memories of September 12, 1995. There is no way to express the violent loss of a child, especially when the perpetrator was a trusted family friend. Memories of September 12, 1995, emerge in her mind's eye when Paulette least expects them. She thinks of McKay. She also thinks about Hilton Crawford, and his memory stirs her anger—she is sure it always will. Yet when memories of the crime and execution enter her mind, she looks over her shoulder for only a few moments. Paulette has learned to live in the here and now and to move forward in a positive direction. It would have been easy to end her life or withdraw from public life altogether.

Paulette chose to persevere. Teaching second graders has allowed her to focus on herself. She had been taught early in life that women do for others. Her whole life revolved around doing for others. Relatives and friends had grown accustomed to her doing things for them. Now in the aftermath of her son's death and the long ordeal that followed, she has to do for herself. While this new-found attitude and spirit has frustrated close friends and relatives, it had to be done. She has "moved on," but on her own terms and not the way others expected.

Friends who did not understand would ask her, "Paulette, didn't Hilton's execution bring an end to this thing? You have to move on—it's time to move on." She wanted to bite the person. She wanted to scream out, "Get real!" and let the person know that nothing ever brings closure to the loss of a child. It was hard for Paulette to understand why people could be so cold. Paulette also questioned whether people wanted her to "get over it" for her own personal well-being or for their benefit.

The treatment of crime victims and the survivors of crimes in American history has, until very recently, been a sad story. Modern society has benefited tremendously from the advancement of technology. People live longer, they eat better, they communicate better, they travel better, and they simply live better than previous generations. The list goes on and on.

One consequence of this improved quality of life and standard of living is the increased pace of life. We have to do everything faster. Six-, eight-, and twelve-lane highways are constructed to carry us to work faster. Computer chips are made smaller and smaller but with increased capacity to process information so we can perform our work tasks faster. Surgical operations are constantly refined so we can heal faster, leave the hospital, and return to work. Virtually everything in modern society has been transformed into faster operations. Those who fall behind are regarded as deviant or out of step.

Crime victims too are expected to "get over it" and the quicker the better. "Seek closure," "Move on," and "Don't let it get you down" represent the common language of most non-victims when advising how victims should respond to tragedy. The treatment of victims in modern American society is a mix. Grief, profound grief, is so raw and difficult to comprehend that most people try not to think about it, much less deal with someone who is grieving. It is uncomfortable to be around grief-stricken people. Funerals today have become ritualized to suit our need for a quick exit from the funeral home and family members. Society at large dictates the terms of grief and loss. Grief must be dealt with fast. A healthy person is one who has shed a tear or two but has jumped back into the game of life.

Some people treated Paulette with respect and dignity through-out the entire ordeal. At other times, she experienced repugnance or was treated as a curiosity. In public settings, even in the last year, it was not unusual to hear, "Hey, that's Paulette Everett, don't you remember her, she's the one whose kid was kidnapped and murdered by a friend? The guy that did it was executed." Yet others have remarked that she needs to "get over it." Paulette felt the larger public wanted her to fake her emotions and adhere to the current social norms about grief and loss—get over it and do it quick and fast. She also felt that people in her community wanted her to "be quiet" and repress the urge to express any rage or anger. People at her church most often took the following position: "Good Christians forgive their enemies and forget, and Paulette has to forgive and forget.

Besides, it has been so long since McKay died, you gotta move on." Paulette thought this position on the part of her fellow churchgoers was ironic and hypocritical—the church was suffocating her in an attempt to bend her spirit for their benefit. Paulette would have none of it and mended her spirit in her own way.

The spirit of the neighborhood where McKay was abducted was also negatively affected. Prior to the kidnapping, the climate there was open, freewheeling, and happy. The neighborhood, when the kids were all outside, had the feeling of being cut off from the rest of the world. Time seemed to stand still. The summers seemed to last forever. It was the definition and picture of innocence. McKay's abduction and murder changed everything. In the days and months after the crime, the children in the neighborhood did not want to be left alone—they did not want to be home without a parent. Many of the parents told Paulette that their children woke up in the night and cried when they thought no babysitter would be present when Mom and Dad weren't home. Soberness rolled over the neighborhood the first year or two after McKay was murdered. Maybe the old spirit of the neighborhood will re-emerge. Time, perhaps, heals everything.

Paulette chose to persevere in mind, body, and spirit, and not give up on life. Her story examined in these pages details one of the most gruesome crimes committed in the twentieth century. The crime rivaled the horrific acts committed by Nathan Leopold and Richard Loeb when they kidnapped and murdered Bobby Franks in May of 1924. The abduction and murder of defenseless children strikes at the core of our conscience. Indeed, such a crime is a parent's worst nightmare.

It would be presumptuous of us to suggest that Paulette's struggle to survive such a loss was an epic worthy of the grandest Hollywood treatment. Her story is no epic of human survival. Every year tens of thousands of Americans are impacted by violent crime. These victims lose their spouses, children, or their friends to horrific and senseless acts of violence. Each case is unique, and the survivors are left to carry on. In many ways the "other" survivors resemble Paulette—many question life, many question their faith, many feel they are on a boat left adrift at sea, many curse their God, many have difficulty getting out of bed each day, many lose their trust in other people, and many wrestle with the meaning of their lives in the aftermath of loss. Although each victim's experience is unique, they do share one commonality—each makes repairs in their body, mind, and spirit, and they keep on living. Paulette has come to realize that life is for the living and you just have to do it.

EPILOGUE

It has been over three years since Hilton Crawford was put to death for the foul deeds he committed in 1995. It's October now, and the weather has finally begun to change. The summer heat has finally left, and people seem to be happy. Cool weather in Texas means football on Friday nights. Stadiums are packed with parents, grandparents, and tons of kids. After the games, the fans pour out of the stadiums to head home. Parents and friends head to the field to see their sons. The players take off their pads and mill around the field discussing the game, key plays, good things and bad.

A lot of the players have girlfriends, and the parents snap pictures to save a memory, to save a moment in time when everything seems right and happy. Plans are made for the next evening. The seniors in the crowd talk about what lies ahead, about plans for college. The game is over and few care about the score. Everybody thinks about tomorrow.

McKay would have been in his twenties today, and maybe he would have played football in high school. Maybe Paulette would have taken pictures of her son after the game and snapped a few shots of McKay with his girlfriend—photographs and memories and albums filled with pictures and cherished moments.

Carl Everett has remarried and has found a new life with someone else. Paulette married Wayne Norman, and she has moved on to a new life. The house where McKay was abducted now has new occupants. The hundreds of bushes and shrubs planted by Paulette and enjoyed by McKay are tall now. New people live in the neighborhood, with new hopes and dreams, new memories, new photos, and happy times. The other kids from McKay's days have grown up and moved on to their futures.

The driveway up to the house looks clean and uncluttered. The paint on the house looks as fresh as the day it was put on. There are cars parked around the back door. Family and friends still use the back door. Some things never change. The sun barely makes its way through the branches and leaves to the surface. This was the path that McKay took when he was first brought to the house. It was a path to a future, a path that was going to be full of memories. It was also the same path that he took on a dark night that robbed him of a future. Maybe, just maybe, the sun can make it through those branches and cleanse the path to a point where futures are possible again.

McKay will never be forgotten, and Paulette will hold on to him forever. Paulette and McKay are attached by invisible strings, mother and child. He was twelve when he was taken away, and he will always be twelve. Mothers never forget, even though they grow older every year. Invisible strings connect them.

The kidnapping and murder of McKay Everett also has deep connections to the victims of the other "Crimes of the Century": Bobby Franks, Baby Lindbergh, Bobby Greenlease, and Baby Weinberger. All of these child victims were betrayed by and then brutally murdered by adults. Their killers were motivated by selfishness and greed. Betrayal and greed, when mixed together, represent the most toxic concoction of all motives for human behavior. Will this cocktail for murder ever be eliminated?

Betrayal and greed and selfishness are part of human existence and will never go away. The acts of Cain, Delilah, Judas, Brutus, and Fredo have been re-enacted a thousand times over, in fact and in fiction. A new year just started. Maybe this year will be different. We can always hope. The antidotes to greed and betrayal are hope and vigilance. Paulette, and other mothers like her, will always be watching.

APPENDIX

Timeline of Significant Dates and Events in the
McKay Everett Abduction-Murder Case

May 1995:

    Hilton Crawford files for bankruptcy in Houston, Texas

August 1995:

    Carl and McKay Everett visit the Crawford residence. McKay plays basketball with Crawford.

    McKay hugs and kisses Crawford as they leave.

September 12, 1995:

    Carl and Paulette Everett attend an Amway meeting at 8 p.m. in downtown Conroe, Texas.

    Around 8:30 p.m., a neighbor observes a gold-colored sedan backing out of the Everett residence.

    Carl calls their residence from a local restaurant several times to check on McKay. McKay does not answer the phone.

    Carl returns home around 11 p.m. to find McKay missing and receives a ransom call. He calls 911 to report the kidnapping.

    Local law enforcement officials and agents from the FBI begin investigation and search for McKay.

September 13, 1995:

    Paulette suffers a stroke.

September 14, 1995:

    A news conference releases first information about the abduction of McKay.

    Hilton consents to the search of his vehicle.

    Irene Flores is arrested and confesses to making the ransom call.

September 15, 1995:

    Hilton Crawford is arrested at his residence at 7 a.m. He confesses to his role in the kidnapping.

September 16, 1995:
    A news conference is held on the front lawn of the Everett residence. Crawford provides directions to the body of McKay Everett.

September 17, 1995:
    McKay Everett's remains are found in a swamp at Whiskey Bay in Louisiana.

September 20, 1995:
    Hilton Crawford is indicted for capital murder.

November 8, 1995:
    Crawford is re-indicted for the capital murder of McKay Everett. Crawford's bail is set at $1 million.

May 3, 1996:
    The trial of Hilton Crawford is transferred to Huntsville, Texas.

July 19, 1996:
    Crawford is found guilty of capital murder.

July 24, 1996:
    Crawford is sentenced to death by lethal injection.

August 9, 1996:
    Crawford's attorneys seek a new trial following a hearing.

September 13, 1996:
    The request for a new trial is denied.

January 20, 1998:
    Crawford's direct appeal to the Texas Court of Criminal Appeals is received.

June 22, 1998:
    Montgomery County District Attorney's Office files its response to Crawford's direct appeal in the Texas Court of Criminal Appeals.

September 9, 1998:
The Texas Court of Criminal Appeals hears oral arguments in Hilton Crawford vs. The State of Texas.

December 15, 1998:
Hilton and Connie Crawford are divorced.

February 17, 1999:
The Texas Court of Criminal Appeals affirms Crawford's conviction and sentence.

May 17, 1999:
Crawford petitions for a writ of *certiorari* in the United States Supreme Court.

October 4, 1999:
The Supreme Court denies Crawford's request.

November 22, 2000:
Crawford files a writ of *habeas corpus* in the United States District Court for the Southern District of Texas.

February 28, 2002:
The Southern District Court denies Crawford's request.

June 24, 2002:
Crawford files an appeal with the Fifth Circuit Court of Appeals in New Orleans.

August 26, 2002:
The State of Texas files a brief in opposition to Crawford's appeal.

December 17, 2002:
The Fifth Circuit rejects Crawford's appeal.

February 11, 2003:
The 9th District Court in Montgomery County (Texas) sets Crawford's execution date for July 2, 2003.

April 1, 2003:

Crawford files another writ of *certiorari* protesting the Fifth Circuit's rejection of his earlier appeal.

June 3, 2003:

The State files a brief in opposition to Crawford's request for a writ of *certiorari*.

June 23, 2003:

The United State Supreme Court denies Crawford's request for a writ of *certiorari*.

July 2, 2003:

Crawford is executed and declared dead at 6:19 p.m.

Last photograph of McKay before he was abducted.